THE
SUPERVISION
SOLUTION:
Manage Performance—Not People

THE
SUPERVISION
SOLUTION:

Manage Performance—Not People

JOHN ROULET

© 2008 Javelin Publishing

Library of Congress Control Number: 2008927304

Roulet, John
The supervision solution: manage performance – not people

Includes index.

ISBN 9780981683768

1. Business - Leadership. 2. Supervision.

TABLE OF CONTENTS

ACKNOWLEDGMENTS

I've listed in alphabetical order the individuals to whom I owe my gratitude for making this book a reality. There are two individuals, however, that I want to list first and foremost, because without them I likely would never have written this book at all.

Deborah Hollis, you are a model of truly great leadership. Your confidence in me and your professional guidance are the two greatest gifts I have received in my career. I will always be grateful and appreciative for having had you as my boss and for having you as my friend.

Randy Simmons, you are one of the kindest and most generous leaders anyone could ever know. I have learned so many important life lessons from you. Your friendship means more to me than you could probably ever imagine.

Anthony Parinello, you were so kind to find the time to provide me with wonderful insights and a kind personal note, even after you must have been exhausted from just completing another of your own books.

Chet Richards, I received your comments and kind words before any of the other experts. When I did, I was as excited as kid at an amusement park. Thank you so much for that moment and all the support you have offered me since.

Clay Howard, your expert artistic consultation during the development of this book was invaluable, as was your kindness and unwavering support.

David Norton, your comments during the drafting of this book and your support offer professional validation that mean more to me than words can express. Your work is continues to be a powerful, enlightening and guiding force for me.

Debra Benton, you seem to know just the right thing to say at just the right time. When I started doubting myself during the final stages of developing this book, you helped me keep my chin up and keep going.

Fabio Camara, thank you so much for the sharing your talents and expertise in providing me with the personal photograph I needed for the book jacket.

Gary Monroe, thank you for taking the time to meet with me. Your insights regarding competitive advantage in a global economy were illuminating and memorable.

Jerry Sternin, the insights you shared with me about Complexity Science resulted in a greater and much needed emphasis on the shared responsibilities of leadership.

Lincoln Adams (the book's illustrator), your drawings brought concepts in the book to life. Your incredible talent and insights provide this book with visuals that are information-packed, memorable and fun. Each and every meeting I had with you was of great personal and professional value.

Linda Mondoux, thank you for your wonderful work, kindness and insights in the proofreading stage of this book. Your work was incredibly fast and complete.

Margaret Cole, as I wrote this book your work as a supervisor provided me with a clear example of what a great supervisor does.

Marilyn Culp, that look you had on your face as you read an early draft enabled me to realize that drastic changes to the manuscript were needed. Your confidence in me and your support mean so much to me.

Michael Lustig, as I first began to write this book you were kind enough to take time out of your schedule to meet with me. The insights and experiences you shared with me about leadership were of great help.

Michelle and Jerry Dorris (the book's cover and interior designers), you both were wonderful to work with. You were kind, insightful and patient throughout the entire process of developing this book. I could not have asked for more.

Pierce Howard, your comments during the drafting stage of this book were invaluable. As a big fan of your work, it was an absolute thrill for me to receive your input and your support.

Rena Henderson (the book's editor), you did an incredible job. I enjoyed and valued every moment of working with you. You make me feel like this book is as important to you as it is to me. Your wonderful writing talents and insights made this book so much better than it ever could have been without you.

Rob August, as I began to develop this book the time you spent with me during a phone interview was enlightening and very valuable.

Robert Mager, your work is wonderful and it has been invaluable to me. Meeting and chatting with you more than a decade ago is still a professional highlight for me. Your comments and kind words during the drafting of this book were of great value.

Steven Yorra and David Lees, thank you for providing me with the sub-title for *The Supervision Solution* and for all of your support.

Toni Roulet, your work in putting together the galley proofs for this book was outstanding. Your diligence, your support and your insights mean so much to me. I'm proud of you and I'm glad you are my daughter.

INTRODUCTION

It is disheartening to see talent and opportunity squandered. Yet, throughout my career, that is exactly what I have seen over and over again. I've witnessed hundreds, if not thousands, of individuals who've gone from having the ability and desire to make great contributions in their organizations, to merely trying to appease their leaders. It is a refrain that is played many times every day and one that has been played throughout history. I wrote this book to do my part to stop it.

This is a book about how to supervise the performance of people in the modern organization. Keep in mind that no matter what kind of business leader you are—whether a CEO of a multinational corporation or a front-line supervisor—if people are assigned to follow you, you *are* a supervisor. And if you are like most supervisors, you've never had a resource that provides you with what you need to master the challenges of supervision. This book is that much-needed resource. It is for business leaders who want more than just ideas. It is for those who want the solutions, once and for all.

It's popular nowadays to think of leadership in terms of individual personality traits and social behaviors. We won't buy into that zeitgeist. A leader can be a compassionate, understanding, dynamic, or even charismatic, but without real leadership knowledge, skills, and tools, he will never demonstrate truly great leadership. Never!

In business, great leadership is *a systematic process* for leading people and driving organizational performance. In this book, you will learn the supervisory component of that process. It is a simple and powerful method that will enable you and your organization to become truly great at managing employee job performance.

All of the principles of being a great supervisor are ready to be discovered. This book will guide you in identifying, learning and applying these principles. Acquiring and applying the knowledge and skills in this book will help you become the kind of supervisor you want you to be—and the kind your organization needs.

You might ask: How is this book different from all the other books that talk about leadership, management, and supervision? What can I get from this book that I can't get elsewhere? There are two key ways in which this book differs:

- First, most of the books about leadership discuss how to change who you are in order to be a better leader and how to change or influence others. Instead, this book not only allows you to be who you are—it urges you to be who you are and to accept that your employees are who they are, as well.

- Second, many of the books on leadership are tomes. That is, they are weighty—both literally and figuratively—books that bombard you with information that is not practical and simply have too many pages for the busy business leader. In comparison, this book is a relatively slim volume. It is not, however, slim on content. It synthesizes information from a wide range of sources to provide you with the most powerful and practical approach to supervision. It is likely to become your go-to resource when you have a supervisory issue or when you want to refresh your memory on some key principles of organizational leadership.

The book unfolds through five sections. The first three sections will provide you with what you need to quickly develop the fundamental knowledge and skills required for every single business leader. Front-line supervisors to CEOs must have this powerful foundation upon which to build all their leadership skills. The fourth section is a how to guide to supervision. It provides you with the information and tools you'll need to efficiently and effectively manage employee performance issues that routinely confound others. The fifth section provides a visual roadmap to becoming a truly great supervisor.

Being truly great at supervision will come quickly to you and to your organization with reasonable focus and diligence. Since leading people is perhaps the most important responsibility any us can have, it is certainly worth the effort.

I hope this book provides you with indispensable guidance and support as you and your organization discover *The Supervision Solution.*

THE CONCEPT OF LEADERSHIP

Section Introduction

If you are in business and you supervise others, you are a business leader. And regardless of the leadership position you hold in your organization, there are some fundamental principles that you must understand. This understanding gives context to the work of leaders so that they can lead much more efficiently and effectively.

This section of the book defines leadership: you can't be great at it unless you know what it is. Amazingly, despite how popular a topic it is, what leadership is remains a mystery to most leaders. Even many of the world's most renowned academic and leadership development institutions operate without clearly defining the concept for students. You and your organization deserve better.

There are two chapters in this section of the book:

1. The Myth and the Truth of Leadership

2. The Measures of Leadership

These chapters provide you with the knowledge on which to build or rebuild the foundation for your leadership skills. That foundation begins with knowing what leadership is and the criteria for measuring the quality of leadership.

CHAPTER 1

The Myth and the Truth of Leadership

At times, it seems that truly great leadership is a mythical concept. Leadership is, however, a very real concept that can be both defined and measured. While the popular view of leadership as an array of personality traits and social behaviors that inspire others has charm, it is not accurate.

We tend to associate strong leadership with individuals who are effective communicators, visionary and inspirational. Our view of leadership becomes hopelessly distorted when it is based on such personal characteristics. Leadership is about work, not personality and social behaviors. As in any work endeavor, an individual's personal traits are an entirely different issue from his performance. The common characteristics associated with leadership are appealing, but they are not synonymous with

3

leadership. This mistake, which is made over and over again, results in the confusing, mediocre and poor leadership we have become so accustomed to in business, government and the military.

THE MYTH OF LEADERSHIP

History provides us with countless leaders who had many of the traits typically associated with great leadership, yet were colossal failures. A recent and notable example comes from the world of business. It is the record of Ken Lay, the former chairman and CEO of Enron.

A former Enron president eulogized Ken Lay as follows: a straight arrow, a "Boy Scout," one who lived by Judeo-Christian principles. These are admirable personality traits and ones that are often equated with great leadership. The many leadership awards Mr. Lay won would seem to validate that view: The Super Hero Honoree Award, The Torch of Liberty Award, Honorary Doctorates in Law and the Social Sciences, Houston Business Man of the Year, Texas Navy Admiral, Chief Executive Officer Award, Father of The Year, and the list goes on.

Given his leadership awards and his $42,000,000 annual compensation package, one could hardly be faulted for believing that Mr. Lay was the stuff of great leadership. However, he was not. His leadership resulted in the collapse of Enron—and with it, the jobs and savings of more than 22,000 employees. The financial and psychological collateral damage that resulted is incalculable. When we consider the true requirements of leadership, as we soon will, it is easy to see that Mr. Lay perpetrated the myth of leadership, rather than the truth of leadership.

THE TRUTH OF LEADERSHIP

Amazingly, it is the 21st Century and we still have nothing close to a universal understanding of this concept called "leadership." Without such an understanding, virtually anything can be considered leadership, and, sadly, it often is. The first step in bringing truly great leadership to any organization is obliterating the confusion surrounding the concept. A simple, powerful and consistent definition of leadership provides the needed foundation:

Leadership Defined

Leadership is the quality of the leader's performance.

It is that simple. Just as workmanship is the quality of the worker's performance, leadership is the quality of the leader's performance.

Measuring Leadership

Three criteria are used to determine the quality of leadership:

1. **Accomplishment**: The leader's performance must result in the achievement of something of value.

2. **Cost-effective use of resources**: The leader must use resources wisely.

3. **Adherence to values**: Whatever the leader accomplishes must be in line with those things that are most important to the group being led.

In the following chapter, we explore each of these measures of leadership in greater detail. For now, let's put a face to the concept and look at someone who was a model of great leadership.

A Model of Great Leadership

Nowadays, we are often presented with examples of leadership that, quite frankly, dramatically miss the point. The common models are CEOs of Fortune 500 companies, military generals and political figures, all of whom command tremendous amounts of resources. Despite the resources they command, their accomplishments often fall far short of what their followers should expect. Their ability to promote themselves often masks less-than-stellar leadership. To cut through the fog of confusion surrounding great leadership, let's consider one of the 20th Century's truly great leaders. Although he was the antithesis of the larger-than-life character associated with so many leaders, he was, in fact, the real deal.

The Mahatma

Born in 1869, Mohandas Gandhi is widely credited with freeing India from colonial rule. When we consider the three criteria of great leadership, Gandhi receives straight A's.

Accomplishment: Gandhi's greatest accomplishment was freeing India from foreign domination. It is for this reason that, in India he is accorded the honor of *Father of the Nation*. His work to the alleviate poverty and liberate women inspired civil rights progress throughout the world.

Cost-effective use of resources: This is, perhaps, what is most impressive about Gandhi. Unlike many leaders, who are allocated massive amounts of money, manpower and technology, Gandhi had virtually no resources in his quest to free India. Amazingly, he even made his own clothes. He led millions of Indians, but these people were not assigned to him. He won them over and they willingly followed him. Gandhi didn't have weapons and technologies at his disposal. Instead, his weapon of choice, which he used with great effectiveness, was civil disobedience. Civil disobedience was not free, however. Many were imprisoned, hurt and even killed for employing this tactic. Still, it is universally acknowledged that, by all measures, the costs associated with freeing India were incredibly low. Arguably, Gandhi was the only person on the planet who could have achieved so much with so little.

Values: Gandhi and his followers, undoubtedly influenced by Hindu philosophy, valued non-violence and truth. It's true that other historical figures founded nations and even did so with minimal resources; however, many fell short when it came to respecting values. What sets Gandhi apart from most other leaders is that his leadership adhered to and even transcended the values of the group he led. Even those outside of his group, including his adversaries, admired those values.

Gandhi's accomplishments, the relatively scant resources he used to achieve them, and the values to which he adhered make him one of history's preeminent examples of great leadership.

THE CRITICAL CONTEXT OF LEADERSHIP

The focus of this book is on the work of leaders—specifically, on the supervisory aspects of leadership. Our definition of leadership, "the quality of the leader's work," does not mean that leadership is an individual responsibility. It is not. *Leadership is a group responsibility.*

No leader or management team can be successful alone. Leaders need the synergy gained when working with others inside and outside of their organization. These include other leaders, subordinates and colleagues. It is impossible to overstate the importance of recognizing and embracing this fundamental tenet of leadership.

Even our example of great leadership, Gandhi, needed thousands, if not millions, of individuals to make his leadership successful. He could not have provided great leadership unless countless others did the same.

CHAPTER TAKE-AWAY

Leadership is the quality of the leader's performance. The quality of that performance is measured by accomplishment, cost-effective use of resources and adherence to group values.

Whether you hold the job of CEO, front-line supervisor, or any other leadership position, this definition and these criteria must always guide your performance.

CHAPTER 2

The Measures of Leadership

I n the previous chapter, we defined leadership and introduced the criteria by which it is measured. This chapter will strengthen the concept
by further explaining the three criteria.

ACCOMPLISHMENT

Goals and objectives are critical terms in the language of leadership.
However, most business leaders understand these terms about as well as
they can understand Sanskrit.

Goals and objectives establish direction. When well structured, they
drive great performance. When poorly structured, they create an over-reli-
ance on hope and chance.

It seems there is a belief that leaders will develop the skills to properly structure organizational goals and objectives through some sort of osmosis—an unspoken presumption that when people become leaders they somehow start providing the organization with well-structured goals and objectives. This common misconception has a costly impact on virtually all organizations.

Goals and Objectives

Goals and objectives are often considered synonymous. They are not. *A goal designates the end of the journey, while objectives are checkpoints showing progress toward a goal.* Objectives must be specific, measurable, achievable, relevant and time-framed. Goals do not have to meet these criteria.

Lost in Translation

Interestingly, in our personal lives, we often demonstrate our ability to structure goals and objectives properly. Yet these same skills are often "checked at the door" in the workplace.

Let's use the example of remodeling a house to see how well we structure goals and objectives outside the workplace. We'll listen in on two discussions between homeowners and their general contractors. The first demonstrates great leadership; the second . . . well, you judge for yourself.

> *Homeowner A: My house is not in great shape. My goal is to have a great house.*
>
> *General Contractor A: Then your having a great house is my goal, too. What does a great house look like?*
>
> *Homeowner A: Three bedrooms, two bathrooms, living room, dining room, electrical systems meet standards, etc. I took one of your own home designs and made some modifications. It's all written down, including the dimensions. So our goal is clear. Do you agree?*
>
> *General Contractor A: Absolutely!*
>
> *Homeowner A: So, let's set some objectives.*
>
> *General Contractor A: We'll have the house gutted in one week. We'll have the frames up in two weeks. We'll have the house finished in seven weeks. We'll go through a "punch list" and have any problems fixed by the end of the eight week. In eight weeks you will have your great house. How is that?*
>
> *Homeowner A: That sounds great. Let's create accountabilities by including those objectives in our contract.*

In terms of goals and objectives, Homeowner A and the General Contractor A have done it correctly. The goal is strong and crystal clear, and there are performance objectives to ensure that everything is done as it should be and when it should be.

Let's now consider Homeowner F and General Contractor F. The discussion below is going to seem absurd; indeed, it is. But what really makes it absurd is that it mirrors what is so common in modern organizations. Activities and confusion abound, and optimal and sustainable performance remains elusive.

> *Homeowner F: My house is not in great shape. My goal is for you to improve it.*
>
> *General Contractor F: We can do that.*
>
> *Homeowner F: How?*
>
> *General Contractor F: We'll fix a lot of things. We'll do a lot of hammering, sawing and rewiring.*
>
> *Homeowner F: I guess that sounds good. Can you give me some timeframes?*
>
> *General Contractor F: Sure! We'll begin hammering and sawing right away. We'll rewire in a few weeks. There is usually high turnover with our workers, so to reduce the turnover we'll be sending some of them to training and others to an off-site seminar. It's all part of our employee development program. So you can see we are going to be very busy.*
>
> *Homeowner F: I guess you know what you are doing. With the money I'm investing and all your activities, it sure seems like the house should improve. When will the work be done?*
>
> *General Contractor F: The work is never done. But don't worry. I'm not going anywhere. You can count on me to stay right here for years to come addressing ongoing problems with our process and workers.*

There are many reasons for chaotic organizational performance and endless problems, but it begins with failing to properly establish goals and objectives. In work environments where people often stay employed by avoiding accountability, setting meaningful goals and objectives is routinely subordinated to job-survival tactics. This kind of environment will never deliver optimal and sustainable performance.

When, however, leaders set goals and objectives that reflect vision and expertise, the stage is set for greatness.

Well-structured Goals

It is not surprising that leaders struggle with structuring high-quality goals. The information available through management texts, classes and seminars is often contradictory and confusing. Let's consider what goals should and should not do.

Goals should:

- **establish broad direction**: "The organization is optimally successful," for example, is a fine goal to have. Any model suggesting that this is not a goal is wrong.

- **provide value**: An optimally successful company is going to provide value to shareholders, customers and employees.

- **later be clarified**: Since an optimally successful organization means different things to different people, the question of what an optimally successful organization looks like needs to be answered. A goal that is not clarified fails to set direction.

The sub-section titled "Putting it All Together," which comes later in this chapter, provides an example of what safe and secure borders look like. You may find it useful to take a quick look at that example now.

Goals should _not_ be:

- **based on improvement**: "Improve company performance" is not a good goal. Improved performance may still result in less than desirable or even poor performance. Improved performance is often just doing things less poorly than they were done before. Improvement goals look backward, real goals look forward. Improvement goals are a common way to tweak the status quo and avoid real challenges and greatness. Improvement goals look backward, while real goals look forward. Improvement goals are a common way to tweak the status quo and avoid real challenges and greatness.

- **constrained by descriptions of activities**: Activities are the way goals are achieved—they are not goals themselves. Including activities in a goal needlessly restricts the path to the goal. "Optimal organizational performance will be achieved by extensive mergers and acquisitions" limits the way the company can achieve optimal performance. There are many other activities that could enable the organization to achieve optimal performance. There is no value in structuring goals that exclude those activities.

- **constrained by timeframes**: In the goal-setting process, there is no value to being needlessly constrained. When it comes time to identify the work necessary to achieve your goal, you'll create objectives with all the timeframes you need. In our present example, our objectives will outline the milestones to achieving the goal of an optimally successful organization. The final objective indicates when the goal will be achieved.

When you look at the "shoulds" and "should nots" listed above, some of them will sound familiar because you've already correctly applied them to situations in your personal life.

Well-structured Objectives

With a goal established and clarified, how to *achieve* the goal takes center stage. That's when you set objectives.

Objectives outline the progression toward a goal and provide the milestones on the path to reaching it. The key to structuring objectives is to make them SMART:

Specific: They must be specific, well-defined and clear.

Measurable: They must be measurable.

Achievable: Since they outline the path to a goal, they must be achievable.

Relevant: They must be relevant to the goal.

Time-framed: It must be clear when they will be achieved.

Putting it All Together

To better understand how goals and objectives relate to one another, consider the following illustration of a goal and objectives that most of us would consider to be of great value.

Goal

An optimally successful organization.

What it Looks Like When the Goal is Achieved

1. Annual profits exceed $5,000,000.

2. 90% of the organization's customers refer at least one client each year.

3. The value of every cause and effect relationship in the organization's business processes is cost-effective.

4. The organization's work environment is productive and respectful (see page 55 for an example of how this is further clarified).

Objectives to Achieve the First Part of the Goal

1. By 12/31/09, our annual profits will reach or exceed $500,000.

2. By 12/31/10, our annual profits will reach or exceed $1,000,000.

3. By 12/31/11, our annual profits will reach or exceed $2,000,000.

4. By 12/31/12, our annual profits will reach or exceed $5,000,000.

The preceding three-part example illustrates the following principles:

1. Start with a goal that is of value.

2. Clarify the goal so that people know what it will look like when achieved.

3. Establish objectives to show the planned progression toward the goal.

This is how great leadership creates the focus necessary to accomplish great things.

This subsection focused on the first of the three criteria of leadership: accomplishment. We'll now proceed to the second measure of leadership: the cost-effective use of resources.

THE COST-EFFECTIVE USE OF RESOURCES

Management requires cost-effectively using resources, and great management is the fuel that drives great leadership. To inspire others or to get elected, leaders will often express their visions of the future. But visions without effective management are not visions at all—*they are fantasies.*

Management Defined

Management is the cost-effective use of resources. This requires minimizing costs and maximizing effectiveness (i.e., achievement).

With unfettered access to abundant resources, anything can be accomplished. But that is not management. Management requires balancing achievement with costs. When something is well managed, resources are not used or sacrificed in excess of what is needed to achieve desired performance. Management requires working costs and effectiveness with equal rigor.

Costs and Effectiveness

To more easily understand the concepts, it is useful to uncouple costs and effectiveness.

Costs include time, money spent, increased risk, lost lives, etc. Costs are incurred with the intent of achieving some level of effectiveness. Effectiveness includes revenue, decreased risk, saved lives, etc. Achievement of a goal is an example of effectiveness.

Management requires balancing costs with effectiveness. Merely cutting costs, a common management theme, as opposed to better *managing* costs, works only one side of the equation: the cost side. A hypothetical business example illustrates this point. Domino's Pizza is a company that many of us know. It would take no management expertise whatsoever to dramatically cut costs at Domino's. All you'd have to do is turn off the electricity and stop buying gasoline for the delivery vehicles, and Domino's operating costs would drop dramatically. Of course, the result of those cost reductions would be no pizzas and no way to deliver those nonexistent pizzas! The company would go out of business quite quickly. So much for effectiveness—but nobody could say that we hadn't cut costs.

On the other side of the coin are achievements under "blank check" conditions. This is where managers consider only achievement, regardless of the cost. Joseph Stalin, the dictator of the Soviet Union from 1922 to 1953, is largely credited with leading the USSR to becoming the second-largest nation in the world in terms of industry by 1937. When viewed in the absence of costs, that is quite an achievement. But, when we consider that Stalin's crash programs of industrialization and collectivization cost the lives of more than 10,000,000 Soviet citizens, the accomplishment loses its luster. Stalin's "blank check" was in human lives. His notorious statement—"A single death is a tragedy, a million deaths is a statistic"—sums up his attitude toward the human currency he spent so freely. His management skills and, therefore, his leadership skills were deplorable.

Merely cutting costs or spending without limit requires no management skills. When, however, costs and effectiveness must be balanced, good management skills are required.

McClellan Versus Lee

The different management approaches of Generals George McClellan and Robert E. Lee provide striking historical examples of poor management—and its tragic consequences—and good management.

McClellan was the Commanding General of the Union's Army of the Potomac in the first year of the U.S. Civil War. McClellan was a compassionate man who loved his soldiers. He was also an excellent organizer. His men were well-equipped, well-prepared and inspired. But as a military commander, McClellan was a horrible manager; he did not know how to cost-effectively use the resources he commanded, and he was hesitant to engage his troops in battle. This resulted in numerous squandered opportunities to win the war quickly. In response to his inaction, his boss, an exasperated Abraham Lincoln, once quipped, "If General McClellan does not want to use the army, I would like to borrow it."

McClellan's counterpart was General Robert E. Lee, Commanding General of the Confederacy's Army of Northern Virginia. As a manager, Lee was the antithesis of McClellan. While he also loved and was beloved by his men, he understood his job and usually performed it with brilliance. He had fewer resources than McClellan, but he used them effectively to achieve a number of great victories for the South.

The contrasting management skills of these two commanders were aptly demonstrated in September 1862 at the Battle of Antietam. McClellan started the battle with superior firepower and almost twice as many troops—and Lee's battle plans had even fallen into his hands. Yet, despite all these resources, the best McClellan could achieve was a draw. Without question, if Lee had been in McClellan's shoes, the outcome of the battle and the duration of the war would have been entirely different. Instead, the battle, which was the single bloodiest day in American history, resulted in a stalemate; the war would continue two and a half more years, needlessly costing hundreds of thousands of lives.

Although the Confederacy lost the war, to this day, General Lee is an iconic figure. This is in large part due to his ability to do so much with so little: a classic example of great management. McClellan, on the other hand, is relatively obscure.

Now that we've considered the first two measure of leadership—accomplishment and the cost-effective use of resources—we'll look at the third measure: adherence to values.

ADHERENCE TO VALUES

We know that great leadership requires great accomplishments and using resources wisely, but that's not enough. Great leaders respect the values of their followers.

Values Defined

Value—or values—is related to worth or importance: What we value reflects what we care most about. When value is made plural (i.e., values), to some this connotes a more ethical concept than the singular implies. We will not make that distinction. Value and values will be used interchangeably.

Consider the following questions: How would you like to turn a $5000 investment into $50,000 in two months? Sounds great, doesn't it? Well, what if the investment involved fronting money for a number of illegal drug deals? Would you still do it? What if there were no chance you would get caught? What if the drugs weren't illegal narcotics, just smuggled prescription medications? Would it make a difference if you needed the money for an operation for a sick child? These are questions of values, questions about what is truly important to you.

The Value of Value

Whether in business, government, or any aspect of life, it is impossible to overstate the importance of the concept of value. Value is the reason why individuals, groups and all species do the things they do, sometimes even without understanding why.

Values are so important that a good number of men have had their presidential aspirations derailed because of their failure to understand voters' values. One recent example is former Senator John Edwards.

In the 2008 campaign, Edwards was positioning himself as the man for the working poor. But his $400 haircut, which was disclosed in his financial report to the Federal Election Commission, seemed to belie that value. No one can be certain if this derailed his campaign, but it is certain that his failure to adhere to the values of the group he wanted to lead severely damaged it. Of course, an expensive haircut has nothing to do with one's ability to lead the United States, but it does make the electorate question your values. That is something even someone with enough money to buy a $400 haircut cannot afford.

On a global scale, there are numerous current value-laden issues. The use of torture on captives in the "War on Terror" raises the question: Is the information that might be gained through torture worth becoming a country that tortures people? Air pollution and universal healthcare coverage are both issues of value. Religions and societies fracture due to discrepant values. Relationships begin and end because of values.

Whether you are a front-line supervisor or the CEO of a multinational corporation, unless you understand and adhere to the values of your group, you will have to retain your position as leader through fear rather than through respect.

CHAPTER TAKE-AWAY

We addressed in some detail the three criteria of leadership: accomplishment, cost-effective use of resources and adherence to values.

Accomplishment is measured by setting and achieving goals and objectives. A well-structured goal is a description of a desired outcome. It is not constrained by the inclusion of activities and timeframes; nor is it anchored by past performance. Goals look forward to a desired state. A goal has power only when it is clarified. Objectives are not the same as goals. Rather, they are checkpoints of progress toward a goal.

Management is the cost-effective use of resources, and great management uses far fewer resources to achieve far more than mediocre management does. Management is a component of leadership, so great leadership requires great management.

Value is related to the importance of something. The leader can accomplish great things and do so by cost-effectively using resources. But if he fails to adhere to what the group values most, his leadership is diminished.

Meeting the three criteria of great leadership at the same time and all the time is the challenge of leadership. Not everyone is up to the challenge, as so many in leadership positions have often shown us.

THE LEADERSHIP SYSTEM

Section Introduction

The first section of this book provided you with a broad view of leadership. In this section, we consider how to best apply that concept of leadership.

In so doing, you'll learn that great leadership skills have limited value unless they are a part of a great leadership system.

There are two chapters in this section of the book:

3. The Concept of a Leadership System

4. The Organization's Leadership System

The chapters will provide you with an overview of the concept of a leadership system and the best leadership system for your organization.

CHAPTER 3

The Concept of a Leadership System

H aving great leadership skills is not enough because a dysfunctional system of leadership can quickly and completely render such talents virtually meaningless.

Leadership development is a popular topic in many organizations. Given its importance to the success of every organization, this is certainly appropriate. Managers attend seminars, training classes and off-site retreats, always with the intention of becoming better leaders. And senior-level business leaders often engage in succession-planning discussions and exercises in which the organization's future leaders are identified and anointed. Even when the quality of such activities is high, the return on these investments tends to be low. New insights and excitement are created, but little meaningful and lasting change occurs.

It seems reasonable to identify and develop high-quality leaders, but this approach continually fails. Why?

ORGANIZATIONS AND SYSTEMS

The approach described above is fundamentally flawed in that it ignores the critical concepts of *organizations and systems*.

The word "organization" is used throughout this book, so let's take a closer look at it. "Organization" is derived from the word "organism." From a biological perspective, an organism is a system of elements that influence each other in such a way that they function as a stable whole. The key concept is that the organism is a *system* of elements, not merely a "pile" of elements. A system brings structure to discrete elements so that they can perform cohesively and productively. The elements themselves often have little usefulness in the absence of this synergistic structure. The effectiveness of systems is why are organizations are created.

The purpose of systems is to provide desired and predictable performance. Systems are all around us. In fact, we depend on them for our survival. The human body is an example of a system that is composed of a number of interrelated sub-systems. If we consider a single human body as a whole system, we see that there are a number of interrelated sub-systems that enable the whole to function effectively (e.g., the circulatory system, the neural system, etc.). A malfunction or weakness in a subsystem will often cause diminished performance or even failure in the larger system. For example, the chronic elevation of blood glucose in the circulatory system can lead to damage of the blood vessels (angiopathy). Damage to other systems within the body will predictably occur.

LEADERSHIP AS A SYSTEM

When we appreciate the value of leadership and of systems, it only makes sense to marry these two concepts in the organizational setting.

When this marriage takes place, thereby forming a leadership system, organizations can realize a synergy and consistency that drives performance to higher and more sustainable levels than can be achieved through the more common individualized perspective of leadership.

It should be noted that the concept of a leadership system is not neces-

sarily exemplified by leadership committees, consensus and other forms of group cooperation. In the absence of a leadership system, such approaches, although well-intentioned, often result in confusion, conformity and ultimately less than optimal performance. These approaches bring leaders together, but they do not typically provide them with the unified set of leadership principles, skills, tools and methods necessary to effectively drive and guide their performance. A great leadership system, however, enables the organization's leaders to perform in a powerful and cohesive manner even when they are not in the same proximity, which should be the vast majority of their time.

The Founding Fathers of the United States

Although not the first group to systematize leadership, the United States' Founding Fathers understood the value of a system of leadership.

Contrary to their era's common model of kingdoms and empires, the Founding Fathers did not leave the future of the United States to a succession of leaders. They knew that to protect the country's future interests, relying on the character and power of individual leaders was not a practical leadership model. What these brilliant men did was to entrust the future of their country to a *system of leadership*, which is outlined in The Constitution. Despite some flaws in the document, the concept of systematic leadership has stood the test of time.

The number of failed dictatorships, kingdoms and empires throughout history that have relied on the omnipotence of leaders instead of a system of leadership further validates the work of the Founding Fathers.

Amazingly, few organizations learn the lessons history has taught us about the power of systematic leadership. Instead many organizations still follow the old-world model of leadership succession and development. The result, virtually by design, is not a system of leadership, but rather a "pile" of leaders. Conflicting talents and agendas and the lack of synergy in this "pile" result in far-from-optimal organizational leadership. Just as a bunch of discrete organs does not constitute a well-functioning human body, a bunch of great leaders does not constitute a well-functioning organization.

The development and implementation of an organization's system of leadership must come *before* the selection and development of its leaders. Thus, the first and most important responsibility of business leaders is to build and maintain a system of leadership for their organizations.

CHAPTER TAKE-AWAY

Regardless of how talented individual leaders may be, this means little or nothing if the leadership system does not support those talents. Business leaders are responsible for building and maintaining a system of great leadership.

CHAPTER 4

The Organization's Leadership System

I n Chapter 3, we discussed the need for a leadership system. The leadership system, which comprises the skills, tools and methods to effectively run the organization, is essential to achieving optimal and sustainable performance. The question now is: What should that leadership system look like? After all, it does an organization little good to recognize the value of a leadership system if it doesn't know what *the* best system actually is. In this chapter, we'll identify that leadership system. Before we do, though, let's consider the biggest obstruction to developing and maintaining an effective system of leadership.

THOSE HUMANS!

The leadership structure in many organizations is more reflective of medieval fiefdoms than of enlightened and powerful leadership systems. Instead of managers behaving as modern business leaders, their actions more closely resemble those of *feudal lords*. Organizational relationships and structures are fractured due to jealousy, incompetence and distrust among leaders. These fractures and the consequent loss of leadership synergy increase costs and diminish effectiveness.

Few organizations would *try* to create fiefdoms. So, the reasonable question is: "Why do they occur?"

Fiefdoms are exactly what we should expect when we put humans together. Since the beginning of our existence, we've lived and worked in clans, tribes, gangs, communities, congregations, fiefdoms, kingdoms, towns, states and countries. In our own lives, we form families, teams, groups, cliques, clubs, etc. That's what we humans do: We are genetically hardwired to create groups. We always have and we always will.

Even our closest genetic relative, the Chimpanzee, forms communities. Like us, they tend to establish territorial boundaries and share resources within the community. Interestingly, one of the notable social characteristics of Chimpanzees is that the males tend to be hostile toward the males of outside communities. Human males, of course, do not behave in a similar manner (a hint of sarcasm, perhaps?).

Status, power and security are things we humans value, and we can attain them more easily by creating subgroups.

Just because humans are predisposed to create groups and exhibit territorial behaviors does not mean that we should merely accept those behaviors. They have a detrimental effect on 21st-century performance, so the issue must be addressed. But any approach that attempts to directly suppress millions of years of evolution is doomed to failure. Instead, what is needed is a leadership system that continually accesses our productive nature, rather than our territorial nature.

THE ORGANIZATIONAL LEADERSHIP SYSTEM

In the early 1990s, David Norton and Robert Kaplan introduced *The Balanced Scorecard*. The Balanced Scorecard is not just a way to manage organizational performance—it is *the* way to manage organizational performance.

It is unlikely that Norton and Kaplan began their work with the intent of controlling our more disruptive prehistoric instincts. But, by discovering the most powerful approach to managing organizational performance, they did just that. A schematic of the model, with modifications to the original, is provided below. We'll soon discuss each aspect of the model and how it drives the other parts of the model.

The Organizational Leadership System

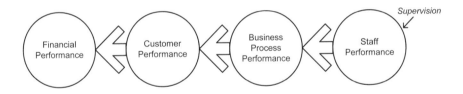

The underlying performance concepts in The Balanced Scorecard direct attention to the behaviors and outcomes that are most beneficial to organizational performance. Of equal importance, the system makes work environments that obstruct optimal performance untenable.

In the management literature, The Balanced Scorecard would be listed under the heading of a "performance management process." The reason for that is simple; it's a process to manage organizational performance.

The Term "Performance Management" Hasn't Caught On

The term "performance management," however, has not caught on with business leaders, and it does not appear that it ever will. Since "performance management" remains an abstract concept to most business leaders, they tend to ignore it or shelve it for another day. I experienced this first-hand when the CEO of a major corporation I was working for stopped by my office one day. I was introduced to him as the director who was developing the organization's performance management process. He offered me a genuine smile and nod of appreciation as he said, "Great, that's what we need." But I could tell that he had no idea what a performance management process was or why it was important to the success of the company. After a few more supportive words, he was gone.

But what if he'd been told that I was developing the organization's *system of leadership*? That certainly would have captured and sustained his attention. He would likely have insisted on being involved.

Few business leaders are particularly excited about performance management. So, it's time to put the term on the shelf for good.

It is a Leadership System

The Balanced Scorecard is a leadership system, and building a Balanced Scorecard is the ideal way for leaders to work with their team to develop a shared vision of the organization. The feedback/review process is an opportunity for the leader to teach and reinforce direction, the cost-effective use of resources and values. This, as we have discussed, is what leadership is all about. In using a Balanced Scorecard, we also see the critical inclusion of others into the process of leadership, a tenet of great leadership. An effective leadership system is one that enables leaders to mobilize people in a focused process of change. Leaders need a system and tools to do this. What makes the Balanced Scorecard so effective is the way it helps to identify, create and sustain the focus. It is *the* leadership system for modern organizations.

Since Norton and Kaplan first introduced The Balanced Scorecard, a number of researchers and practitioners, including myself, have made modifications to the model. The model described in this book reflects the modifications I have made. Regardless of the changes, the basic tenets of the Balanced Scorecard remain intact. Norton and Kaplan's work is brilliant in the power and relative simplicity it brings to driving optimal and sustainable organizational performance.

Henceforth, I'll use the term *leadership system* rather than The Balanced Scorecard. I'll do so in deference to Norton and Kaplan's work and their use of the term "performance management system."

The Four Parts of the Leadership System

One of the real benefits of a leadership system in an organization is that it moves leadership from a theoretical construct to a real, practical and workable one.

Historically, organizations have relied almost exclusively on financial measures to manage performance. Whether it is our bank accounts, portfolios, or credit card debt, such measures of financial performance provide us with information about our past decisions and actions. The same holds true for the financial measures organizations use. These measures provide insight into the quality of *past* decisions and actions.

Therefore, additional measures are needed to understand, predict and capture the future. These additional measures are customer performance, business process performance and employee performance.

These are the four components of an organization's leadership system. Performance in each component of the process is driven by the ones that precede it:

1. **Financial performance** is of value because money enables the organization to survive and thrive and satisfy its shareholders.

2. **Customer performance** provides value to the organization based on the sales realized from customers purchasing its products and services.

3. **Business process performance** provides value to customers by providing the products and services they want.

4. **Employee performance** is of value because it makes the business process work.

The performance/value relationships described above are the heart and soul of the leadership system. Effective leadership aligns and drives each component of the process.

*The purpose of this book is to provide organizations and their supervisors with what they need to develop the **employee performance** component of the leadership system.*

MANAGEMENT JOBS

In a great leadership system, job titles have meaning beyond symbols of power and status. Instead, they designate in which part of the leadership system the leaders' accomplishments will occur.

If you have ever seen preschoolers play soccer, you've seen them pile up as they chase and kick the ball. The coach has little chance of keeping them in their assigned positions. It's adorable!

Many managers perform in much the same way; they come together and pile up on a business issue. They do a poor job of staying in their assigned positions and, thus, effectiveness and efficiency suffer. It's not adorable!

As was discussed in the last chapter, there is no value in managers piling up on a problem. Yet, it is not uncommon to see vice presidents, directors and managers join together to spend hours fumbling over a personnel problem that a single supervisor should have handled in a few minutes. Effective leadership systems do not allow leaders to pile up on a problem. Instead, each leader has a distinct job and set of responsibilities. Leadership is driven by expertise, as opposed to power or the number of leaders.

Leadership systems must provide a clear understanding of business leaders' roles in the organization. This is not merely a description of activities and lines of authority. Business leaders' roles must be structured to be far more powerful than that. The jobs of business leaders must be structured in terms of their *deliverables* to the organization. In other words, what are the performance outcomes and value of their responsibilities? In Chapter 9, you will learn the method for determining the value of specific

jobs. You can apply this method to learning the value of every job in the organization.

Job titles will vary from organization to organization. In the model below, the most common management job titles are used to show the distinctions in leadership responsibilities/deliverables:

- **Vice Presidents through CEOs** have organization-wide policy and financial responsibilities. The principle performance deliverables of these jobs are measured in terms of the organization's *financial performance* and the quality and alignment of its entire leadership system.

- **Directors** are responsible for strategy. This requires making decisions and taking the actions necessary to position the organization in the minds of customers or other key stakeholders. Performance deliverables might be measured in terms of market share and other strategic measures. These jobs are also responsible for the quality and alignment of the *customer performance* component of the leadership system.

- **Managers** are responsible for developing, transforming and maintaining the organization's *business processes*. The performance deliverables for these jobs are measured in terms of how cost-effectively products and services are provided. They are also measured in terms of the quality and alignment of the organization's business processes.

- **Supervisors** are responsible for ensuring optimal and sustainable *employee performance*. Additionally, they are responsible for the quality and alignment of the organization's process to manage employee performance.

Leadership jobs will often carry responsibilities that require performance across several components of the leadership system. It is not uncommon, for example, that a talented director is solely responsible for strategy, building a business process and supervising staff.

Since the focus of this book is on supervision, we'll continually emphasize ways to ensure optimal and sustainable employee performance.

Assigning Job Titles

Appropriately assigning managerial job titles has little to do with administrative niceties. It is a matter of clarifying leadership purpose and accountability. Identifying and distinguishing between the management deliverables helps prevent talented individuals from moving into leadership jobs for which they do not have the skills.

With regard to supervision, for example, many talented employees who are promoted into supervisory positions don't have the skills it takes to drive optimal and sustainable staff performance. But, since most organizations don't have a clear idea of what supervision entails, this leap of faith is common. A great system of leadership, of course, does not accept this approach to staffing.

CHAPTER TAKE-AWAY

In the absence of a strong leadership system, organizational fiefdoms will evolve. A great leadership system obliterates costly fiefdoms and replaces them with a systematic approach to achieving optimal and sustainable success. Such success is achieved by aggressively managing employee performance, business process performance and customer performance. The value of effectively managing these aspects of performance is reflected in the organizations' financial performance. The organization's management jobs have specific performance requirements that are directly related to each of the four components of the leadership system.

As you consider your job within your organization's leadership system, it is important to determine and fulfill your role as a leader in building and maintaining that system. *The Skills, Tools and Methods of Supervision* section of this book provides "nuts and bolts" to build and maintain the staff performance component of the leadership system.

APPLIED LEADERSHIP

Section Introduction

The first two sections of the book took us from the broad concept of leadership to how organizations systematize leadership. We'll continue to narrow our focus, as we now look at how business leaders actually lead.

It's popular and even a little charming to view business leaders as great motivators. In reality, such individuals are rare and not necessarily effective leaders. To be a truly great business leader, one must have real leadership *knowledge and skills* and, of course—as discussed in the previous section of the book—work within a great leadership system.

Great leadership in business requires managing performance by creating and maintaining work situations in which talented people will thrive. To do this requires the most powerful and practical problem-solving approach in the universe.

There are three chapters in this section:

5. What Business Leaders Manage

6. Great Leadership Changes and Maintains Situations

7. The Universe's Problem-solving Method: GIADA

In these three chapters you'll learn some of the most valuable lessons of business leadership. They will enable to you to develop the skills you'll need to develop your foundation for all levels of business leadership. And, again, since out focus is on supervision, you will be applying these foundational leadership skills to managing the performance of people.

CHAPTER 5

What Business Leaders Manage

An organization's leadership system is designed to manage performance. Virtually everything a member of management does is for the purpose of achieving desired performance.

PERFORMANCE

Managers at all levels manage performance. Supervisors manage staff performance. Regardless of their position in management, if leaders do not know what performance is, they cannot manage with optimal effectiveness.

Performance Defined

Performance is two things and two things only: behaviors and outcomes.

43

Employees are hired to behave in a certain way and to achieve certain outcomes. Essentially, this comes down to two types of directives:

1. Do it this way. (behaviors)

2. I don't care how you do it; just make sure it's done. (outcomes)

Some management teachings identify performance outputs and outcomes. My finding is that output is an additional performance category that creates unneeded complexity. It is easier to combine outputs and outcomes into one category: outcomes. Goals and objectives, which were discussed earlier, are examples of outcomes.

Employees can often achieve outcomes through a multitude of behaviors. Thus, a business leader may allow an employee a choice of behaviors and measure the employee's performance solely on the outcome achieved.

Manage Performance, Not People

Leadership books and articles frequently suggest ways to manage people. This is patently incorrect. Cult leaders manage *people*, but business leaders manage *performance*. Skilled business leaders do not try to manage personalities and emotions because they know they do not have the time or psychotherapeutic skills to do so. Their job, instead, is to ensure that necessary organizational behaviors and outcomes occur.

The Issues of Personality and Emotion

Research shows that certain personality characteristics, such as conscientiousness, are associated with higher levels of performance. That, however, does not mean that supervisors have the time or skills to instill or develop such traits in employees. Supervisors' attempts to increase organizational performance through pseudo-psychological interventions are not only flights of fantasy, but they also are ethically questionable.

Certainly, people in some jobs, such as office receptionist, are required

to offer friendly greetings and to be polite. It seems reasonable to expect individuals in such jobs to be cheerful. Cheerful, however, is an emotion or a personality trait; it is not a performance. Regardless of a receptionist's emotional state, the job requirement to offer friendly greetings and to be polite does not change.

Many of us at any given time will be dealing with issues such as divorce, death, financial problems, etc. Consequently, we may not feel the positive emotions a manager wants us to feel. That, however, does not mean that we won't perform our jobs with great effectiveness. We humans are very adept at performing well in spite of our emotions.

The work of the business leader is to manage performance, not personalities. Often, supervisors' attempts to change or control employees' emotions and personalities result only in confusion, frustration and diminished performance.

VALUE

Performance is only as important as the value it provides to the organization. As discussed earlier, value is importance or worth. Great performance does not always equate to value, a premise that many companies, such Ford Motors, have learned the hard way.

Shortly after being named of CEO of Ford Motor Company in 2006, Alan Mulally, cited Ford's earlier failure to recognize fast enough that the public no longer valued SUVs as much as they did prior to the dramatic increase in gasoline prices since 2004. Ford's SUVs, such as the Explorer and Expedition, were of high quality. But since fewer people wanted to buy them, they had little or even negative value for Ford. Mulally states that Ford's anticipated return to profitability will be largely due to the company's ability to better recognize what customers value and what they do not.

Leadership requires creating performance and value links throughout the organization. Each component of the leadership system is designed for exactly that purpose. Value is what drives and guides performance. Value is the reason why certain performances must occur and why others must not.

CHAPTER TAKE-AWAY

Performance is behaviors and outcomes, not personality or emotions. What makes performance important is the value it provides. Value answers the question as to why performance is required or not required.

Leaders all too often misunderstand or ignore the concepts of performance and value, but embracing and understanding these concepts are crucial to truly great leadership.

CHAPTER 6

Great Leadership Changes and Maintains Situations

Business leaders manage performance, and that often requires employees to adapt to change. Change, however, is not accomplished by trying to manage people; it is achieved by managing the situations in which people work.

Many CEOs are frustrated by their management teams' inability to embrace needed change. Important changes are often compromised or abandoned when managers resist change and even subvert activities that threaten the status quo. Common ways to deal with managerial behaviors that obstruct change include speeches, cajoling and attitudinal training. Yet these approaches rarely, if ever, result in desired and sustained performance changes.

THE CONCEPT OF CHANGE

Although well-intentioned, attempts to get employees to embrace change are rarely necessary. It's a waste of time to try to alter employees' attitudes about change—it doesn't work, and, even if it did, such attitudinal changes do not result in better organizational performance.

When necessary organizational change fails, the problem is not within the collective minds of employees. It is in the situations in which they work. When employees obstruct change, it is because the work environment is weak and not conducive to success.

In the past 80 years, the human relations school of management has dominated discussions about business leadership. Its approach encourages leaders to understand followers' feelings and perceptions. Such an understanding, if it can be achieved, is said to guide the speed and the degree of change the organization can handle. The approach sounds somewhat sensible, but it is naïve; it fails to appreciate the proven strengths of humans.

Humans are Great at Adapting to Change

Throughout history, people have adapted and even thrived in difficult and unexpected situations. The story of our species is one of adaptation. Some extraordinary and less extraordinary examples are useful to drive this point home.

Immaculee Ilibagiza, a survivor of the Rwandan genocide of the 1990s, tells a remarkable story of how she and six other women were huddled in a bathroom, measuring three feet by four feet, for 91 days while they hid, sometimes only a few feet from rampaging mass murderers. They were forced to take turns standing and stretching during their ordeal. Food was scarce to non-existent. They survived.

Members of the military have always had to adapt to extreme situations. Refugees and the hundreds of millions of citizens who toiled and starved under the regimes of Mao Zedong and Joseph Stalin are examples of mass populations that adapted to ungodly situations. Pioneers and explorers endured hardships most of us can hardly envision.

Examples abound of people surviving under the harshest conditions, but survival is only one factor in humans' ability to adapt and thrive. Among the many other reasons people adapt are religion, love and loyalty.

Even many of us pampered souls of the 21st century are quite adept at adapting and thriving in the midst of change. How about mothers? Talk about adapting to change! They adapt to having a human being growing in their body for nine months and then to being responsible for their baby's survival. Every day, people adapt to changes brought about by death, divorce, sickness, job loss, etc. Parents respond to continual changes in family life as their children grow and move out of the house. Whether our ability to adapt to change was a creation of God, evolution, or both, modern organizations are left with nothing meaningful to teach employees about how to better adapt to change.

The Status-Quo Bias

People tend to resist change. There is no question about that. Our tendency to resist change, however, does not imply that we're anything less than great at adapting to it. On the contrary, our ability to overcome fear and apprehension makes our accomplishments that much more impressive. Unfortunately, business leaders too often botch change efforts because of misguided attempts to do battle with our natural tendencies.

Our tendency to resist change is known as the *status quo bias*. Insights from the field of evolutionary psychology provide a rational explanation for this bias: embracing the status quo was, for our prehistoric human ancestors, very much a requirement for survival. We modern humans are the products of our cave-dwelling ancestors. These early humans faced incredibly harsh conditions; weather, geography and predators presented challenges to their survival each and every day. Those who would venture into unknown environments, particularly alone, dramatically decreased their chances of survival. In such conditions, those who were wet, cold and hungry, but *relatively* safe in the confines of a cave surrounded by fellow clan members, were more likely to pass on their genes than those with a proclivity to venture into the elements. Consequently, those traits associated with accepting the status quo would be passed on, while those rejecting it were systematically eliminated from our gene pool.

Like virtually all other higher-order species, we humans have a particularly strong desire not to lose what we already have. In the case of our species, it is a cognitive phenomenon that is aptly called *loss aversion*. Loss aversion is the tendency for people to put greater importance on losses than on gains. Before taking actions that could result in gains, we first tend to weigh the risks of loss very heavily. The fierce desire to avoid losing what we already have has been essential to the survival of our species. We protect what we consider to be ours, most notably our food, our shelter and our families. Some of the common behaviors associated with loss aversion are hiding, hoarding, threatening and fighting. Although these may seem like primitive behaviors, almost all 21st-century organizations regularly provide numerous examples of hiding, hoarding, threatening and fighting behaviors in humans.

Although it can be a severe obstacle in our modern world, the desire to resist change is still very much a part of our genetic make-up.

GREAT LEADERSHIP CREATES AND MAINTAINS NEEDED CHANGES

It is, as we just discussed, fruitless to try to change the way people *feel* about change. What the successful leader will do instead is to create and maintain a work environment in which talented individuals will be allowed to thrive

Remove the Shackles

Far too often, work environments misdirect, restrict and obstruct great performance. In such environments, the organization's leaders are actually preventing great performance instead of driving it. Unclear direction,

ineffective communication and chaotic business processes are among the many reasons that prevent talented employees from delivering great performance. The impact is increased costs, decreased effectiveness and lost opportunities. It is, therefore, of paramount importance for business leaders to destroy the shackles that prevent great performance as quickly as possible.

Creating Change is One Thing, Maintaining it is Another

Rather than stopping at merely creating change, the responsibility to *maintain* needed change adds a substantially different dimension to the leader's work. Change can be created very quickly and very dramatically—bombs and tornados, for example, create dramatic changes. But bombs, unlike humans, can neither decide what changes to make nor maintain those changes. Only great leadership can purposefully create and then maintain needed change.

An event on May 1, 2003 provides a striking example of a leader failing to understand the distinction between creating change and maintaining it. It was on that day that President George W. Bush flew onto the USS Abraham Lincoln and declared the end of major military actions in Iraq. He announced this as he stood beneath a sign that read "Mission Accomplished." As we know now, contrary to those proclamations, major military actions did not end and the mission had not been accomplished.

Still, by May 2003, Iraq had changed, and it had changed dramatically: Saddam Hussein was no longer in power; his military was crushed; and many Iraqis experienced a sense of freedom and exuberance as they had never before. This situation did not last, though. The reason: those who planned the war failed to plan for peace.

For the President, as the leader of the free world, accomplishment should have been peace and freedom in Iraq. This required recognizing that the goal was, indeed, a peaceful and free Iraq, not just the overthrow of Hussein's dictatorship. The next step was to clarify this goal. If that goal were to be pursued, objectives outlining the milestones and timeframes toward goal achievement were needed. Such an approach is the work of great leadership, and it always will be.

For the business leader, the lesson is that creating change is typically much easier than maintaining it. Great leadership requires understanding and preparing to maintain change *before* creating it. Without this level of preparation, leaders are likely to lose control of situations that could have been effectively managed.

A Work Situation a Business Leader Might Create and Maintain

It is, as we discussed, fruitless to try to change the way people *feel* about change. What the successful leader will do instead is create and maintain a work environment in which talented individuals will thrive, even in the face of change. The bulleted statements below describe such a work environment. It is an environment that a business leader may choose to create and maintain. The list could even serve as a promise to the organization's employees.

- *Each employee knows what needs to be accomplished and why. All the work can be linked to helping the organization achieve its desired market position.*

- *Each employee has the information and tools necessary to perform his/her job effectively.*

- *The courses of action taken are well planned and understood, such that forces obstructing desired performance are routinely avoided or defeated.*

- *Everyone on staff performs at or above what is outlined on their performance appraisal. Performance deviations that are below requirements are addressed quickly, systematically and fairly.*

- *Members of the group are not treated disrespectfully by anyone in the organization, and the work environment is not de-motivating.*

The fourth section of this book, *The Skills, Tools and Methods of Supervision*, will give supervisors what they need to systematically create and maintain such a work environment.

CHAPTER TAKE-AWAY

Employees do not have to be coddled, cajoled, or coerced to adapt or to thrive in quality work environments. Great leadership drives optimal and sustainable performance by creating and maintaining work environments/situations in which talented employees will thrive.

CHAPTER 7

The Universe's Problem-solving Method: GIADA

G reat leadership requires disciplined thinking. Leaders must be organized and fast in their thinking so that they can make timely and correct decisions and then take relentless action. GIADA is what enables leaders to do just that. GIADA stands for **goal**, **information**, **analysis**, **decision** and **action**.

GUNSLINGERS AND SHAMANS

Too frequently, a "shoot from the hip" mentality is more common among managers than is high-quality thinking and action. Instead of engaging in a systematic process of problem solving, managers jump right to a solution without clearly understanding if there is a problem and what its causes and impact might be. The inevitable result is confusion, wasted time, increased costs and decreased effectiveness. When business leaders are asked to outline their approach to problem solving, their responses, more often than not, cite an intuition or a "feel." There is nothing wrong with intuition and feel. They are important. But they are not foundations for problem solving and are more appropriate for gunslingers and shamans than for modern business leaders.

Great leadership requires using the same problem-solving model that all higher-order species appear to be born with. Leaders choosing to ignore

the rules of our universe do so at their organizations' peril. The problem-solving rule that comes with our universe is GIADA.

GIADA and Two of the World's Great Competitors

The First in the Wild

Imagine a tiger in the wild. She needs to eat. Therefore, right now, food is her **goal**. GIADA is how she will ultimately achieve that goal. She's surrounded by **information**, some of which she collects and some of which she ignores. There is a field mouse about ten feet away; a large deer grazes 100 yards away in a clearing; and a smaller deer grazes 50 yards away near some high grass. She **analyzes** the situation. She could catch the mouse, but that wouldn't be much of a meal; she'd expend more energy catching the mouse than it is worth, and she'd alert the deer to her presence. The large deer would be a great catch, but there's a good chance it would escape before she could get to it. The smaller deer, however, is near some high grass that she could use for cover, and she doesn't have to traverse as much ground to get to it. She makes her **decision**. She's going after the smaller deer. She takes **action**. She stalks her prey through the high grass. The moment she sees the deer alert to her presence, she pounces. In the space of about 40 yards and eight seconds, the hunt is over. She has achieved her goal and she will eat today. GIADA at work!

The Second on Ice

Some may argue that leaders in the modern business world simply don't have time to structure goals, collect information, analyze the information, make the right decisions and then take the appropriate actions. Time, they would argue, sometimes does not allow for GIADA. This, however, is utter nonsense.

The process of setting a goal, collecting information, analyzing it, making a decision and taking appropriate action can take less than one second. Wayne Gretzky is a perfect example of a leader who understood and embraced GIADA.

It is generally acknowledged that Wayne Gretzky was a highly-skilled ice hockey player. He did not have the best shot, wasn't the fastest skater or the strongest person on the ice. He was, however, the greatest at GIADA. Gretzky was aware that when he was on the ice, his team's goal was to score. At any moment, he was collecting all the relevant information on the ice. Much of this information would change numerous times within a matter of seconds. He analyzed the information in microseconds and made decisions that no one else even saw as options. His decisions led to the quick actions that often resulted in his team scoring a goal. Gretzky had the best mind the game of hockey has ever known. Relative to hockey, GIADA was likely Wayne Gretzky's greatest strength.

GIADA is what we've been given as the most effective way to think and act. There are no shortcuts! And, of course, most business decisions will not be made as quickly as Gretzky's. Nevertheless, the process remains the same. And the process is not entirely linear—it requires looping back to prior steps until the goal is achieved. Information will change as decisions are made and actions taken; assumptions upon which decisions were made will sometimes be wrong; and the goal may change as new opportunities emerge and disappear. Such changes are common and are a part of GIADA.

A supervisor, like a tiger and a hockey player, needs more than good intentions to effectively work through GIADA. The following section of the book, *The Skills, Tools and Methods of Supervision*, offers just that. With those skills, tools and methods, you will be able to work through GIADA to create and maintain a high-performance work environment.

CHAPTER TAKE-AWAY

GIADA is the most efficient and effective way to make decisions and take actions in an organization. GIADA often requires looping back to prior steps as changes occur. Leaders must always be flexible enough to reconsider their goals, information, analysis, decisions and actions.

GIADA is not a "flavor of the month." Whether in your personal life or business life, it is the most effective approach to problem solving.

THE SKILLS, TOOLS AND METHODS OF SUPERVISION

Section Introduction

E ach day, the performance of billions of employees is managed by supervisors who rely on their wits and vague organizational guidelines. Many supervisors quickly realize that the skills that made them successful in non-managerial jobs will help them little in supervision. What they need is an entirely new set of knowledge, skills and tools—one that equates to supervisory expertise. In this section of the book, you'll learn both what supervisory expertise is and how to use it to be a great supervisor.

The first three sections of this book discussed leadership concepts. This section continues to narrow our focus on leadership. Here, we will address the "nuts and bolts" of supervision.

Since supervision is managing people's performance, it has a prominent place in the organization's leadership system model.

The Organizational Leadership System

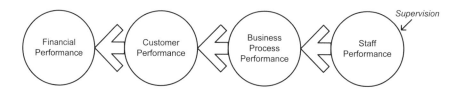

Supervisory expertise requires understanding what it takes for humans to perform a job effectively. That understanding begins with the seven-step job performance model outlined below—it is the foundation for supervising people. Note that the model is cumulative—that is, each step is dependent upon all the steps that precede it.

THE JOB PERFORMANCE MODEL

Information $\Rightarrow$ Knowledge $\Rightarrow$ Skills $\Rightarrow$ Tools $\Rightarrow$
Motivation $\Rightarrow$ Effort $\Rightarrow$ Performance

- *Information*: Individuals need information to understand the job to be performed.

- *Knowledge*: Information is transformed into the knowledge of how a job is supposed to be performed.

- *Skills*: Knowledge, often through practice, is used to develop the skills to perform a job.

- *Tools*: Knowledge and skills have little value unless the proper tools are available to perform the job.

- *Motivation*: The desire to use information, knowledge, skills and tools to perform.

- *Effort*: The energy one puts into performing a task.

- *Performance*: The behaviors and outcomes that occur as a function of information, knowledge, skills, tools, motivation and effort.

As you look at your own job, or any job you supervise, you should see the natural flow of these steps. The model, like much of the material in this book, is somewhat intuitive. As a supervisor, you must get comfortable with this model so that you can allow each member of your team to progress smoothly through the steps. This model is supervision!

In the upcoming chapters, you will learn how to create and maintain a work environment in which a smooth flow through this model is the norm for the group you lead.

There are nine chapters in this section:

8. The Best Possible Performance Appraisal

9. The Value of Job Performance

10. Providing Employees with What They Need to Perform

11. Documenting Performance

12. Motivated Employees Do Not Have To Be Motivated

13. Analyzing Job Performance Problems

14. Resolving Job Performance Problems

15. Punishment

16. Hiring Employees that Provide Needed Value

These chapters will provide you with information and tools necessary to effectively manage staff performance. When you apply all the concepts you will learn in these chapters, you will bring truly great supervision to your workplace.

CHAPTER 8

The Best Possible Performance Appraisal

Many business leaders question the value of performance appraisals to their organization. They see it done inconsistently, and the process does not appear to deliver any significant return on their organization's investment.

In reality, the importance of performance appraisals is widely accepted—even by those who publicly dispute their validity. We see performance appraisals every day in, for example, the sports pages of every major newspaper. The performance measures used include batting average, points per game, rushing yardage, etc.

If performance appraisals are not important, then it is time to stop counting strokes in golf and to take the numbers off the bathroom scale. The reality is: *performance appraisals are important.*

A great performance appraisal, which you will learn to develop in this chapter, is the foundation for great supervisory performance.

PERFORMANCE APPRAISALS MEASURE JOB PERFORMANCE

Performance appraisal isn't about the employee; it is about the employee's performance. Telling employees the sort of people they are (e.g., "You're a bulldog" or "You're a go-getter") does not constitute a valid appraisal of their performance. It is not the kind of information an organization can effectively use.

Accurately measuring employee job performance is as important to organizational success as measuring financial performance. A CEO would never collect and use information about the company's financial performance in the sloppy manner that employee performance information is typically collected and used. When done correctly, measuring employee

job performance is easy to do, requires little time, is very accurate and can be used to drive overall organizational performance.

Why We Struggle to Assess the Performance of People

People categorize people. It's a natural thing for us to do, and it's as much a matter of survival as of convenience. Humans assess individuals and situations in microseconds to determine whether or not they are a threat. This is made possible by the way our brains collect, code and categorize information. If we take a moment to describe our boss or some other associate, we quickly see the natural tendency to categorize people. Our description will likely include one or more traits (e.g., smart, talented, arrogant) rather than a list of behaviors and outcomes. This is how our brain saves us time and effort. Instead of considering thousands of observations before determining what kind of benefit or threat a person is, a relevant category immediately comes to our conscious mind, summarizing most of what we know and feel about that person. To do anything other than categorize people requires suppressing our natural tendencies.

Categorizations

Although categorization is an efficient way to process information, it has severe limitations in today's business environment. The categories in which we place individuals have an emotional association. Thus, our judgment of an individual will be influenced by the emotion associated with the category. Further, in the work environment, the emotion will tend to bias the assessment of performance in the direction of that emotion.

So, if someone is categorized as dishonest, a clearly negative category, we are likely to judge that person negatively. The converse is also true. The positive emotions associated with a category, such as pleasant, will likely result in a favorable judgment of someone we deem pleasant. These emotional responses pose a big problem when it comes to accurately measuring performance. For example, thinking of a person as very nice or very attractive can severely bias our assessment of that person's performance.

In such cases, the performance is frequently assessed to be better than it actually is. We humans are not constructed to filter out our emotions in order to easily process performance information.

This information-processing bias became abundantly clear to me a number of years ago. I used to play softball on an excellent team. Carl was a teammate who I considered to be a poor outfielder. I would view any good play he made as an anomaly. In my young and arrogant point of view, he was a selfish person for not accepting the role of designated hitter instead of playing outfield. "Selfish" was the category Carl occupied in my brain. One day, my girlfriend at the time told me that every time I came to bat, Carl would cheer loudly for me. I told her that was utter nonsense because that's not the kind of person Carl is; selfish people do not do such things. She told me to listen next time I went to the plate. So I did. She was right! Carl was cheering loudly for me, perhaps more loudly than anyone on the team. Not only that—I realized that I had heard that same encouraging voice over and over throughout the years. Yet I failed to connect those cheers to Carl because they were incongruous with my categorization of him as selfish. It was only after I consciously discarded my negative categorization of him that I was able to collect and analyze relevant performance information accurately. The result was that I was finally able to see that he was actually performing well in the outfield and was a great teammate. It was a lesson I hope to never forget and one that I hope you will also remember.

Once supervisors accept their natural tendency to categorize people, they can overcome it: They can use a performance appraisal process that measures performance, and only performance.

How to Develop Great Performance Appraisals

To assess performance correctly, you'll likely need to forget much of what you've learned. Performance appraisal does not measure personality, potential or anything other than past performance. The right performance appraisal is job-specific; it is not a generic form. It makes little sense, for example, to assess the performance of a person who cleans our car by such generic measures as teamwork, leadership and initiative. Instead, we would use performance measures such as how shiny the exterior is; how clean the windows are; and if what we were told about price and timeframes was accurate. This same rule of *measuring job performance based upon required behaviors and outcomes* applies to every job.

The Ideal Performance Appraisal

	Doesn't Meet Expectations	Meets Expectations	Exceeds Expectations	Weighted Rating
Takes complete patient history, including events leading to current visit, prior illnesses, and other relevant information.	❑	❑	❑	30
Provides comprehensive examination relevant to the chief complaint.	❑	❑	❑	25
Develops an accurate diagnosis.	❑	❑	❑	25
Develops proper treatment plan taking that considers issues of patient compliance, effectiveness, cost, pain reduction and recovery time.	❑	❑	❑	20
Overall rating	❑	❑	❑	

The performance appraisal above is an example of what might be created for a family physician job. The structure of this performance appraisal is ideal. It clearly outlines expected performance and the relative importance of each performance component. It is possible to create levels of performance in addition to the three listed here. My experience, however, is that this is typically unnecessary.

By putting the appraisal in a spreadsheet or a database, with some relatively simple calculations, the process can be fully automated to score each appraisal and to combine performance information across many jobs in the organization. It also takes less than a minute to complete.

How to Create the Ideal Appraisal

Step 1:   Choose a job for which to develop a performance appraisal.

Step 2:   Generate a list of performances (behaviors and outcomes) that must occur for the job to be performed as required. Most jobs include five to seven performance requirements.

Often, it is impossible to identify everything that must occur in a job. In such cases, an item can be included that leaves some supervisory discretion. It's not as good as having everything defined ahead of time, but it is reality.

Step 3:   For each performance requirement, determine what the range of acceptable performance is. This range is based on value; how to do this is addressed in the following chapter.

Step 4:   Determine the relative importance of each performance requirement. When they are all added together they must equal 100%.

Step 5:   Make sure that all staff members have a copy of their performance appraisal. This is necessary information for them to perform their jobs effectively.

Step 6:   Use the appraisal regularly to assess the performance of each staff member.

CHAPTER TAKE-AWAY

You and your organization can be great at measuring employee performance. It's relatively easy when done correctly. Well-constructed and regularly-used performance appraisals establish the foundation for great supervision.

There is some flexibility in the structure of performance appraisals and how performance is measured (e.g. frequency, quality, quantity). But performance appraisals must always meet the following three criteria if they are to be considered ideal:

1. Each component of required job performance must be clear.

2. How well each component needs to be performed must be clear.

3. The relative importance of each component of job performance must be clear.

CHAPTER 9

The Value of Job Performance

Why does a given job exist? What is the impact on the organization when the job is performed great versus at a mediocre level? What would happen to the organization if the job were to go away? Organizations that capture and effectively use such valuable information are rare. Unfortunately, rather than meaningful measures of value, anecdotal information regarding the value of jobs tends to be the norm.

At all levels, supervisors typically define their jobs as making sure others do *their* jobs. This is not an unreasonable description. But for supervision to be most effective, both the supervisor and the organization must understand the value of the jobs being supervised. It is only with this knowledge that an organization can determine whether a job should exist and, if so, what levels of performance are acceptable.

ALIGNING VALUE WITH PERFORMANCE

The performance appraisal describes desired performance. But, as we've discussed, performance is not enough. It is necessary to understand the *value* of performance. The appraisal is the starting point for determining the value of a job and varying levels of performance within that job.

The Value of Varying Levels of Performance

Does great performance or mediocre performance really matter in a job? The answer to that could be yes, or it could be no. It requires supervisory expertise to make that determination. It is quite possible, for example, for a ten-percent difference in the productivity of two employees to deliver substantially discrepant levels of value. The value of processing 12 bills per hour as opposed to 10 bills per hour might be $50,000 per year for an organization. In highly technical and management-level jobs, the value difference in varying levels of performance can increase exponentially.

The Return on the Organization's Investment

Organizations invest their resources in jobs in a number of ways. Employee compensation is typically the most costly of these ways.

Although compensation tends to be driven by what the labor market is paying, knowing what a job will return on an organization's investment enables the organization to determine how aggressively it wants to compete for employees in the labor market. Understanding the value of performance allows leaders to make such proper hiring decisions and to determine resource allocations and employee compensation levels.

HOW TO IDENTIFY THE VALUE OF A JOB

The purpose of this process is to identify the range of acceptable performance for each component of a job. This range is based upon what the supervisor determines to be acceptable differences in the value of the high end of acceptable performance and the low end.

Step 1:   Start with the performance appraisal.

Step 2:   For each job responsibility, determine whether performance is measured based on behavioral frequency (e.g., how often a customer is greeted as required) or on an outcome (e.g., number of sales).

Step 3:   Identify the highest level of performance that has ever been observed. The highest level may be unattainable to all but a few gifted individuals. This step is designed to direct attention toward greatness. It is probable that this level is too high to serve even as the high end of acceptable performance, but it creates a better frame of mind for setting that standard.

Step 4:   Identify the high end of acceptable performance and the value associated with that level of performance.

The value will likely be in terms of money, reduced risk, and/or legal compliance.

Step 5:   Identify the low end of acceptable performance and the value associated with that level of performance. Once again, the value will likely be in terms of money, reduced risk, and/or legal compliance.

Step 6:   Compare the difference in the value between the high end of performance and the low end.

Step 7:   If the range is too big, make the range smaller. This is usually done by increasing the level of the low end of performance, not decreasing the high end.

Step 8:   Document for the organization why you set the performance ranges as you did. Let's say, for example, that you identified the difference between the value of the low end and the high end to be about $5000 per year. Briefly explain why that difference is acceptable to the organization.

CHAPTER TAKE-AWAY

Varying levels of performance typically have varying levels of value to an organization. If people were robots, perhaps it would be reasonable to have a single point of acceptable performance. But people are people, so performance will vary. Based on the value lost and gained, the supervisor must determine the amount of variation the organization can handle.

CHAPTER 10

Provide Employees with What They Need to Perform

I t is all too common for employees to be hired into jobs and then left to figure it out for themselves. That's not empowerment, as some may suggest. It is supervisory negligence.

Talented employees need knowledge, skills and tools to perform. Surprisingly, business leaders often either overlook or ignore these critical components of the job performance model. The result is always diminished organizational performance.

TAKING CHARGE OF THE SITUATION

People rarely start their jobs with all the knowledge, skills and tools they need to be optimally successful. While a high-quality selection

process results in new hires being productive faster, employees will still need help acquiring the essentials to achieve optimal performance. If supervisors fail to fulfill this responsibility, they court real performance problems for their organization.

General George Patton was a great supervisor who ensured that his team had the knowledge, skills and tools required for success. After the Americans' disastrous WWII defeat in March 1943 at the Battle of the Kasserine Pass in North Africa, Patton was given command of the Army's II Corps. When Patton took over, the II Corps was in physical and emotional tatters. Within weeks, as a result of intense training and discipline, the II Corps was on the offensive and pushing German and Italian troops out of North Africa.

Due to the immense size of an army corps, Patton could not personally train and equip his troops. But he made sure that it was done—and done right. His example provides two critical leadership lessons:

1. The supervisor must take responsibility for his subordi-
    nates' acquisition of knowledge, skills and tools.

2. Regardless of the size of the group, this responsibility
    must somehow be met.

When a supervisor fails to take charge of the learning process, employees may learn needed skills too slowly or not at all, and organizational
performance and value will suffer.

How to Provide Performance Essentials

Step 1:   Create a picture of performance for each item
            on the performance appraisal. This is known as a "task
            analysis." The easiest way to do this is to sketch a simple
            flow chart. If you are unfamiliar with flowcharting, it is
            relatively easy to do if you keep it simple—which you
            should. The Internet has a number of useful references
            that can immediately provide you with the information
            you need. Below is a partial example for a performance
            requirement from the physician's performance appraisal
            in Chapter 8. The task analysis is for the following job
            responsibility: *Takes complete patient history, including
            events leading to current visit, prior illnesses and other rel-
            evant information.* The task outlined below begins when
            the doctor first meets with the patient.

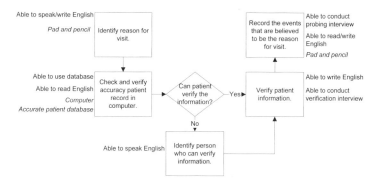

Step 2:   Next to each step, identify the knowledge, skills and tools that you, as a supervisor, must ensure that the incumbent has to perform that step of the job.

Step 3:   In a separate place, clarify the knowledge and skills identified in the task analysis. For example, "able to speak English" might be clarified as *able to speak English at a high school graduate level.* "Able to use database" might be defined as a*ble to retrieve and print all patient information from the patient database.* Clarity regarding exactly what the organization needs is the critical issue here.

Step 4:   Of the knowledge and skills identified, determine the ones that employees do not yet have.

Step 5:   Structure a cost-effective approach to ensuring that the proper knowledge and skills are learned and maintained. Provide, if appropriate, job aides, feedback and guidance.

Step 6:   Now that the employees have the knowledge and skills to begin performing their job, make sure that they have the tools to use that knowledge and those skills with optimal effectiveness. So, get those tools in place.

If the organization cannot provide all the tools, communicate this to the employee and make adjustments to the performance expectations, if appropriate.

Step 7:   Now, use your performance appraisal and documentation skills to monitor and measure employee job performance.

CHAPTER TAKE-AWAY

As a supervisor, it is your responsibility to ensure that knowledgeable and skilled employees have the tools they need to perform their jobs with optimal effectiveness. Employees expect supervisors to create and maintain this kind of work environment. When this doesn't occur, performance will never be optimal. Never!

CHAPTER 11

Documenting Performance

Once you have developed performance appraisals and know the value of performance in each job, the employees that report to you will have clearly defined performance expectations. Of course, employees now are going start performing. As their supervisor, you need to monitor their performance.

As time goes by, you are not going to accurately remember all your observations of job performance. That's why you'll have to document performance. Most business leaders realize that they should document employee performance, but, in truth, few do. Documenting employee performance is probably the most boring of all supervisory tasks, and many business leaders consider it the least important. Nevertheless, it is a leadership task that must be performed. The good news is that when done correctly, it should only take a few minutes of your time each week.

OUR COGNITIVE LIMITATIONS IN THE MODERN WORLD

Supervisors need to document performance because the human brain cannot accurately store and recall the information needed to assess the performance of a single employee, let alone many. Failing to properly store and recall performance information has resulted in countless poor performers retaining important jobs they had no business keeping. In such cases, leaders are likely influenced by information that is unrelated to performance. This happens when memories, instead of brief written performance notations, are used to store, code and retrieve performance information. These memories, as we discussed in the performance-appraisal chapter, will be skewed due to the categorizations our brains make. Taking a few moments per week to document subordinates' job performance helps maintain a much-needed focus on *performance*.

How to Document Performance

Fact files are logs of performances and assessments of those performances. To keep easy and up-to-date fact files, use the performance appraisal. When performance is above or below what is expected, the supervisor should make notations and initiate a brief discussion to determine the reason for such deviations. The following are included in each note: the date, the situation, the performance and an evaluation of the observed performance. The evaluations must be about the performance, not about the employee. The key is to imagine being in a court of law: Nothing in a fact file should be anything less than a fact. Let's consider two sample fact files, one good and one not.

- Good: August 4, 2008: Employee was given four reports to complete today. He completed only two. Everyone else in the group completed all four of their reports under identical circumstances. Employee's performance was unacceptable for this assignment.

- Not good: August 4, 2008: Employee was given four reports to complete today. He completed only two. He's not meeting his potential.

The "good" fact file entry describes and assesses the employee's performance. The entry marked "not good" also describes the employee's performance, but assesses the employee instead of his performance.

Chapter Take-away

Documenting performance is a necessary task of supervision. When the performance appraisal is used as the basis for maintaining documentation, the task is simplified and is far more accurate. The documentation provides a journal, or log, of employee performance that would otherwise be forgotten or distorted. The information in this journal provides the supervisor with what he needs to complete accurate performance appraisals and to have ongoing and meaningful performance-related discussions with employees.

CHAPTER 12

Motivated Employees
Do Not Have To Be Motivated

Nowadays, there is so much discussion about motivating employees. Granted, motivation is a critical component of the job performance model. But what supervisors often fail to recognize is that the talented employees on your staff should *already* be motivated.

IT'S THE ENVIRONMENT

It is a myth that supervisors need to motivate employees. The cause of motivational deficits will not be found within the people on your organization's payroll. The sad truth is that a good number of dedicated and talented employees find their work environments de-motivating.

Work is often more about job survival than about delivering truly outstanding outcomes. In such environments, behaviors that could improve organizational performance are often subordinated to those that cause minimal disruption to the status quo. The work environment becomes permeated by the need to conform rather than the need to perform. Supervisors who are in tune with the needs of quality performers recognize that their focus must be on the work environment, not the individual psyches of employees.

Conformity

Groupthink, a concept whereby disagreement with the leader is punished and conformity is rewarded, is a common and destructive example of this get-along mentality. In many organizations, the negative consequences associated with failing to conform include the loss of promotion opportunities, being accused of not being a team player and even job termination.

The effect of groupthink is so strong that many social psychologists blame it for the escalation of the Vietnam War. When important decisions were being made about the United States' involvement in Viet Nam, most of the men on President Johnson's staff withheld expert opinions that conflicted with the president's views. These conflicting opinions would, no doubt, have been of great value to the country. Unfortunately, the desires of these influential men to be viewed favorably by the president and to retain their positions of power had tragic consequences.

Conformity at the expense of performance is always detrimental to optimal success.

Treating the Symptoms Does Not Work

In recent years, there have been a number of popular and questionable approaches to motivating employees. Such approaches seem to assume that employees are in a collectively depressed emotional state that can be resolved through interventions such as training, pep rallies and parties.

If there is a genuine lack of motivation in the work environment, the proper approach begins with understanding why—i.e., a diagnosis. The diagnosis will inevitably identify the work environment, not the collective psyche of employees, as the problem. Thus, any intervention should aim to alter the environment, not to *fix* the employees. When employees appear "depressed," they often are, in fact, simply adapting to a dysfunctional work environment.

Most people come equipped with the motivation to do good work. Self-esteem, survival, family security, social acceptance and status are among the many factors that make us naturally motivated to perform. When supervisors believe that they need to motivate employees, they fail to appreciate and, perhaps, even respect the people who report to them.

The supervisor's task is to structure and maintain a work environment that does not subvert employees' natural motivation to perform. Humans and, thus, organizations thrive in such an environment.

How to Structure the Work Environment

There is no textbook way to create a work environment that does not de-motivate. There are, however, a few principles for structuring an environment that drives performance rather than suppressing it. Four simple and powerful principles are of particular value: positive reinforcement, negative reinforcement, punishment and extinction. Although the names of some of these principles may be unfamiliar, we all know how the concepts work.

- Positive reinforcement: A behavior is increased based on the belief that a reward will follow. If an employee receives recognition for getting a report in on time, we can expect that the behaviors associated with generating sales will increase.

- Negative reinforcement: This is also a rewarding experience. However, instead of getting something good for demonstrating a behavior, something bad is avoided or taken away. If, for example, an employee can avoid the wrath of his supervisor by getting a report completed on time, the behavior of getting the report completed on time is negatively reinforced.

- Punishment: Punishment is not a rewarding experience. Its purpose is to decrease or eliminate an undesired behavior. If an employee actually experiences the wrath of his supervisor for submitting a report after deadline, the behavior of turning reports in late will likely decrease or be eliminated in the future.

- Extinction: Extinction is also not a rewarding experience, and, like punishment, it results in a decrease in a certain behavior. A behavior is extinguished when nothing happens after its occurrence. If a weekly report is generated and nothing happens with the report, we can expect that the behavior of generating that report to cease in time.

Great leadership makes sure that the work environment does not punish or ignore desired performance and also does not reward performance that is detrimental to organizational success. For example, it is not uncommon for an employee who once showed a willingness to help out with an unpleasant task to get stuck with the task from that point forward. In this case, the employee is punished for helping out. Honesty is also often punished in organizations, as is taking responsibility for errors. Self-promotion, on the other hand, is often rewarded, while hard and smart work is ignored. Supervisors must understand that employees' performance, whether good or bad, has consequences. The work environment must be structured in such a way that desirable actions are rewarding and undesirable ones are not. This is how supervisors take control of work environments.

CHAPTER TAKE-AWAY

With regard to motivation, preventing de-motivation is the critical responsibility of the supervisor. Great leadership requires structuring the work environment so that it does not de-motivate. Trying to get employees pumped up to work is usually unnecessary and has no lasting positive effect.

CHAPTER 13

Analyzing Job Performance Problems

The process of resolving job performance problems requires a systematic approach to defining the problem, determining its impact, diagnosing causes, and choosing and implementing a cost-effective solution. It's GIADA through and through. You may want to go back to Chapter 7 for a quick review of GIADA.

When performance appears to fall below desired levels, common managerial "knee-jerk" responses include increased oversight, retraction of authority, increased hiring and more training. Rarely do these approaches fix the underlying causes of performance problems. They are merely band-aids that address symptoms. Prolonged problems, increased costs, and decreased effectiveness are the inevitable outcomes of such myopic leadership.

AVOID MANAGERIAL MALPRACTICE

A doctor who prescribed a course of treatment without first under-standing the cause of a medical problem would clearly be engaged in mal-practice. Yet such short-circuited problem solving is common in business and government. Too often, leaders jump in with costly and unnecessary solutions. This is largely the result of not understanding the nature of problem. Effective problem solving requires understanding a problem, identifying treatment options, choosing the best treatment option and

acting to resolve the problem. Problem solving is how leaders create solutions.

Leaders Provide Solutions, Not Just Ideas

Unless a performance intervention is the result of systematic problem solving (GIADA), it is merely an idea, not a solution. Ideas are fun, but there are already zillions of them out there. Great leaders transform ideas into meaningful solutions.

Resolving job performance problems cost-effectively requires a fast, powerful and systematic approach. The successful supervisor starts with the job performance model:

$$\text{Information}\Rightarrow \text{ Knowledge } \Rightarrow \text{ Skills } \Rightarrow \text{ Tools } \Rightarrow$$
$$\text{Motivation } \Rightarrow \text{ Effort } \Rightarrow \text{ Performance}$$

The cause of any job performance problem will be found in one or more of the components of the model. Always!

How to Analyze Performance Problems

The need to analyze and resolve a performance problem begins when performance dips below the required level. The performance appraisal will provide that measure of performance. Due to the associated loss of value, performance problems should be addressed immediately.

The supervisor's answers to the twelve questions below provide the needed analysis to understand the problem, its impact, its cause and the options to resolve it.

1. What is current performance?

2. What *should* it be?

3. Is there a performance gap?

4. If so, what is the impact of the gap on the organization

in terms of wasted resources, lost opportunities, safety and legal compliance?

5. Is the problem worth fixing?

6. Is the problem a function of information, instruction, or tools that an employee should have but does not?

7. Is the work environment structured in such a way that it does **not** de-motivate desired performance?

8. Does the employee have everything necessary to succeed?

9. If the employee has everything necessary to succeed, what additional steps will be taken to ensure that the employee will be successful from this point forward?

   In many cases, the answer may be "none." Everything reasonable may have already been done. If something can be done, a performance achievement plan (PAP—see next chapter) should be developed and implemented.

10. Given the impact of the current performance problem, how and when must the problem be resolved?

11. What are the costs to the company of the chosen resolution and the timeframe?

12. How will desired performance be maintained?

These questions form the basis for a plan of action to get individual and group productivity where they need to be. The plan must include the following;

- a clear description of the performance problem

- the costs associated with the problem

- how and when the problem will be resolved

- the cost of that resolution

- how desired performance will be sustained

CHAPTER TAKE-AWAY

When the performance of an employee is less than that outlined in the performance appraisal, the supervisor must take a systematic and aggressive approach to diagnosing the cause of the problem and quickly resolving it. A comprehensive performance analysis, such as that outlined in this chapter, is invaluable to enabling supervisors to do just that.

CHAPTER 14

Resolving Job Performance Problems

Supervisors often resign themselves to having some employees who don't quite carry their weight. Despite numerous discussions about performance, little seems to change. Although performance that doesn't meet the requirements is disruptive and frustrating, in many organizations this is considered an unavoidable workplace reality. This is sheer nonsense!

In the previous chapter, we analyzed job performance problems. We'll now address how to resolve performance problems when an employee has all he needs to perform as required, but is not. This is where Step 9 of the performance analysis in Chapter 13 comes in: the performance achievement plan.

PROPERLY FRAME THE PROBLEM

Few people savor interpersonal conflict. It can cause feelings of distress for all parties involved and can result in the initiator being ostracized from a relationship or a group. Avoiding interpersonal conflict can be negatively reinforcing: by avoiding conflict, an individual can avoid distress and the threat of being ostracized and, thus, the perceived loss of comfort and relationships. The very human desire to avoid interpersonal conflicts is the very reason why many performance problems are not addressed until they become absolutely intolerable.

No Conflict is Necessary

The good news about resolving job performance problems is that no confrontation is necessary when it is done correctly.

Dealing with an employee whose performance is not meeting standards is relatively easy when the issue is properly framed: the employee's performance is not where it needs to be; there is an associated loss of value; and you'll do what is reasonable to help fix the problem.

If your job performance analysis revealed that the performance discrepancy is the result of a shortage of information or tools, the problem would reside with you, the supervisor. You would be responsible for providing that information and those tools or for changing performance requirements to account for those missing performance essentials. Through your analysis, however, you have determined that the employee has all he needs to perform as required, but his performance does not meet the levels required. The problem has a cost and must be resolved. When an employee has the same understanding about the problem as you have, there is little need for conflict. So, resolution can and should proceed quickly.

HOW TO DEVELOP A PERFORMANCE ACHIEVEMENT PLAN (PAP)

Resolving a job performance problem begins with a performance achievement plan for the underachieving employee. The plan is not puni-

tive. It is the organization's sincere attempt to assist an employee in getting his performance where it needs to be so that termination can be avoided.

If the employee can bring his performance back to the required level and sustain it, then a written plan can be avoided. If not, the supervisor must develop and implement one immediately.

There is a lot of science and a little art to developing the plan. Sometimes, supervisors will find that a few well-chosen words can make the plan feel a little threatening, and at other times they may want to keep it soft. This is entirely a matter of feel and will change from plan to plan.

Regardless of the tone, supervisors should never structure plans that result in the following:

- improvement gains that fall short of desired levels;

- timeframes for improvement that are too long and, consequently, too costly;

- reduction of individual performance expectations to better fit the capabilities of an underperforming employee.

Elements of the PAP

1. What is current performance?

2. What *should* it be?

3. Is there a performance gap?

4. What is the impact of the gap on the organization in terms of wasted resources, lost opportunities, safety and legal compliance?

5. What additional steps will be taken to ensure that the employee will be successful from this point forward?

   In many cases, the answer may be "none." Everything reasonable may have already been done.

6. Given the impact of the current performance problem, when must the employee's performance reach competency?

   Important: The greater the loss of value to the organization, the shorter the timeframe for reaching competency.

7. What are the consequences for not reaching acceptable performance within the timeframe given?

   The consequences must be aimed at getting performance back on track, not punishing the employee. This is true even if the consequences are termination from the job. In such a case, termination is not an act of punishment; it is the action needed to remove an employee from a job for which he is not a good fit. This serves to protect the interests of the organization, which is being hurt by the employee's unacceptable performance.

8. What are the costs to the company of the chosen resolution and the timeframe?

9. How will performance be sustained at the new level?

A *PAP* does not require confrontation. It is a fair and systematic approach that is for the benefit of the employee and the organization. Supervisors should, therefore, do their best to understand and to communicate it in just that way.

CHAPTER TAKE-AWAY

When performance, as defined on the performance appraisal, falls below required levels, a performance achievement plan may be required for an employee. This plan is relevant only when the employee has been provided with the essentials to perform and still is not performing as required.

CHAPTER 15

Punishment

E uphemisms such as "progressive discipline" do not alter the fact that organizations do punish employees. It is, at times, necessary. Unfortunately, instead of a systematic and mature process, many organizations use an undisciplined and, at times, unsophisticated approach.

Supervisors are often exasperated with what it takes for a problem employee to be fired from their organization. Even with records of poor attendance, insubordination and misconduct, some employees are still allowed to keep their jobs. Oral warnings, written warnings and suspensions have little impact on employees who seem determined to disrupt the work environment. As a consequence, the work place is diminished, and supervisors feel helpless rather than empowered.

PUNISHMENT PROTECTS WHAT THE ORGANIZATION VALUES

"Progressive discipline" is the common term organizations use when they want to punish an employee. It is, however, a misnomer because to be disciplined is a good thing. Being disciplined means that we follow a beneficial rule of conduct. Most of us would like a little more discipline in our lives. If we had such discipline, we might exercise more, eat better and be more patient. Employees who are disciplined thinkers are critical to the success of an organization. So discipline is good thing. To be punished, on the other hand, is not. None of us strives to be punished.

Punishment is appropriate in organizations and always will be so long as they are staffed by people. People misbehave. In response to human transgressions, The Bible and The Koran prescribe pretty severe punishments. Needless to say, no one would suggest that an employee be stoned for committing an infraction of company policy. Still, we can't ignore the fact that appropriate punishment does stop undesirable behaviors and does have its place in business.

Punishment is Only for Violations of Policy

Punishment is never appropriate for performance problems—only for policy violations.

Policies reflect what the company values. When an employee violates policy, we want that behavior to stop and to never occur again. Therefore, punishment, in the form of an oral warning, a written warning, or termination, may be appropriate. Such actions protect the organization's values. An organization's response to policy violations provides insight into just how fiercely it protects its values and its employees.

Punishment and Shame

Although punishment is an organizational reality, good leaders understand its emotional impact on employees and their productivity.

There is the very real possibility of causing a punished employee to feel some degree of shame. And shame is a very powerful feeling. Countless people have chosen death over living in shame. Even today, there are societies that endorse the killing of women for acts considered shameful. Even under the best of circumstances, employees who feel shamed by organizational punishment may withdraw from the organization (i.e., quit) or demonstrate a drop in productivity.

Theory of the Mind

To gauge our standing in relationships, we reflect on what others are thinking. This is called theory of mind. Such reflections benefit us in that they guide us toward behaviors that maintain or improve our standing in a social structure and away from those that would threaten it. People are likely to avoid behaviors that violate group norms and thereby bring punishment.

Talented and well-meaning employees are likely to be stigmatized by punishments such as written warnings or job suspensions. Although such punishments are rarely public, they are still likely to be interpreted as organizational "badges of shame." Like a "scarlet letter," they mark employees as transgressors of organizational values.

Employees with written warnings or job suspensions on their records are commonly marginalized by the organization; they are often unable to apply for other jobs until a certain amount of time has passed since their punishment. Despite an employee's understanding that the punishment was fair, the strong desire not to be a marginal member of the organization can drive the shamed employee to seek other opportunities where he can start anew. Withdrawal from a community or a society is a very human response to condemnations received for violations of accepted norms.

There is evidence from recent neurological research that shows that the neurons in our brains reconfigure to better retain memory of events that are both atypical and traumatic. Such events, therefore, achieve greater prominence in the human brain. For many employees, punishment and its associated shame is such an event.

Clearly, because employees will reflect painfully on the event, leaders must use punishment judiciously and with expertise.

Punishment in Well-led Organizations is Rare

The talented people who are on the payroll in well-managed organizations will have no desire to violate policies. Thus, policy violations will likely be minor and can be addressed by a quick discussion; written warnings and suspensions tend to be unnecessary overreactions in such environments.

Punishment in Well-led Organizations can be Harsh

Well-run organizations have little time or tolerance for nonsense. Therefore, in such organizations, wanton policy violations can easily result in termination. This is the way such organizations protect their values, their employees and their reputation.

How to Punish Employees

Great supervisors recognize that punishment is an after-the-fact remedy: the problem being addressed has already occurred. For this reason, supervisors must create a work environment in which there is no need or desire to violate policies. But when violations do occur, guidelines and a systematic process are required address them effectively.

Guidelines

- Any time an employee is punished, identify the consequences for further violations of policy.

- Punishment must be progressive. Never go backwards (written warning to oral warning) or sideways (written warning to another written warning).

- Combine policy violations when considering an appropriate level of discipline. For example, you can combine excessive absenteeism and insubordination. They both come under the category of disrupting the work environment.

- Don't create a statute of limitations.

- Don't use suspensions. If an employee has done something bad enough to warrant a suspension, he shouldn't be on the payroll. It would be best to terminate employment.

- Be consistent.

- Violating policies is entirely separate from performance. How well a person performs is irrelevant to organizational punishment. If, for example, an outstanding performer sexually harasses a co-worker, this is no less serious than a mediocre employee engaging in the same conduct.

- Never use compromise punishments. They only assure that the wrong level of punishment will be administered.

- The entire situation must always be considered. The exact same violation can be rewarded in one circumstance and result in termination in another. If an employee falls asleep at his desk because a crisis required him to work 24 hours straight, that probably does not violate the organization's values. Someone who sneaks way from his job in the middle of a crisis to grab a nap, however, is another case entirely.

- Use the word "punishment" because that's what it is.

The Process

Step 1.   Determine, in behavioral terms, what should have or should not have occurred.

Step 2.   Identify, in behavioral terms, what occurred.

Step 3.   Identify the policy violation (e.g., insubordination, misconduct).

Step 4.   Determine what the maximum level of punishment could be for that policy violation.

Step 5.   Collect background information (reasons, history, etc.).

Step 6.   Determine what the impact, or potential impact, will be on the organization if the policy violation happens again.

Step 7.   Determine whether punishment needs to oc
            cur to prevent the violation from happening
            again. If so, decide on the level of punishment.

Step 8.   Take action.

CHAPTER TAKE-AWAY

Organizational punishment is designed to immediately stop unwanted behaviors. It is appropriate only when addressing violations of policy, and not when addressing performance. Punishment has an extraordinarily powerful impact on talented and well-meaning employees, who are the only ones that should be on the payroll. Punishment should, therefore, be used with great expertise.

CHAPTER 16

Hiring Great Employees

Perhaps, despite being on a PAP, an employee's performance still did not meet requirements. Consequently, he was terminated from his job. Or maybe he was terminated for a serious policy violation. Or, maybe, he just decided to leave the company. Whatever the reason, now, assuming that the organization still requires the job to be performed, someone has to be hired.

Unfortunately, to the detriment of creating real value, the approaches of most organizations to hiring and promoting employees reflect art much more than they do science. In making hiring decisions, supervisors and HR representatives will frequently rely far too heavily on their belief in their ability to *read* people. But relying on such primitive skills is a desperately outdated way to assess qualifications for 21st-century work.

HIRING THE RIGHT PERSON IS IMPORTANT

A powerful 1990 study by Hunter, Schmidt and Judiesch validated the importance of hiring the right people. Some of their more potent results were that the in medium-complexity jobs (e.g. clerical jobs with some decision-making responsibilities) the top one percent of performers were 85-percent more productive than average performers. That means it takes almost two average performers to equal the work of one top performer. The performance variability between the top one percent of employees in medium-complexity jobs and those in the bottom one percent is a startling 12 to 1 difference. Sales jobs and high-complexity jobs showed even greater variations. If there were ever any doubt, their data clearly illustrate the value to organizations of hiring the right employees.

IT'S NOT REALLY ABOUT COMPATIBILITY

An interviewer may believe that he has the ability to choose the right candidate based on a gut-level feeling—that belief, however, is erroneous.

The basis and the impact of this misunderstanding have received substantial attention in organizational psychology. What has been found is that gut-level feelings do not reliably lead to good hiring decisions. Instead, such feelings are more likely to result in selections that are based on applicants' compatibility with the interviewer.

We humans are hardwired to choose individuals with whom we are compatible. While our feelings and instincts serve us relatively well in choosing companions, they can interfere with our ability to select qualified employees. Substantial research shows that our personal feelings about applicants' physical appearance, gender, race, age, college attended, etc. impair our ability to objectively assess their qualifications.

We can all cite numerous examples of individuals who were hired and promoted for reasons clearly not based on their skills. In many of those cases, the hiring managers' subjective perceptions guided the selection process.

Since leaders tend to pride themselves on their instincts, it has always been nearly impossible to convince them that their gut-level feelings are far less effective than a well-structured employee selection process. Employee selection based on compatibility and affiliation has a long and tragic history in business, government and the military. Unfortunately, due to our strong desire for compatibility, the legacy will continue for a long time to come. However, organizations that can overcome this natural tendency will be well positioned to dominate those that can't.

How to Hire Great Employees

Three Important Definitions

1. **Ability** is the capability to do something. People may not yet have the knowledge or skill, but they have the ability to learn and develop them.

2. **Knowledge** is the understanding of how something is supposed to be performed. Knowing how to do something does not necessarily translate into being able to do it.

3. **Skill** is being able to perform. A skill is not performance. A person can have skills, yet choose not to perform. The distinction between skills and performance is an important one: It is not uncommon for less-skilled individuals to outperform those with higher skill levels. Greater motivation, intelligence and persistence can overcome skills discrepancies.

When considering the qualifications of job applicants, your primary responsibility is to measure their abilities, knowledge and skills. To do this effectively is a two-step process: 1) develop the selection process and 2) use it.

Develop the Selection Process

Step 1:   As usual, start with the performance appraisal. The appraisal outlines the job requirements and their relative importance.

Step 2:   Refer to the task analyses you created to identify the knowledge, skills and tools employees need to perform this job with optimal effectiveness (see Chapter 11).

Step 3:   Identify which knowledge and skills the new hire must have on day one to perform as required. You will be testing to make sure that applicants have these skills.

Step 4:   Since you may not be able to assess each applicant on all the knowledge and skills required to perform the job, select the ones that are most important for success in the job and the ones that are hardest to teach.

Step 5:   For the knowledge and skills in which you've decided to assess applicants, identify ways to determine whether or not each one has that skill. Usually, the person will have to *demonstrate* the skill to you.

Step 6:   Develop the kind of test and/or questions that will enable you to determine that each applicant has the requisite knowledge and skills. Three methods will help you do this: behavioral interview questions, situational interview questions, and skills tests.

Behavioral Interview Questions

These questions require applicants to reference situations in which they have personally been involved and to paint a picture of what their performance looked like in previous jobs. These questions enable you to venture into their past. You should use behavioral interview questions whenever you can assess qualifications based on applicants' prior experience.

Patterns, Patterns, Patterns

A common, but incorrect, type of interview question begins with, "Tell me about a time when. . . . " The question is weak because it requires applicants to identify only a one-time example of great performance. Even the most incompetent employees can point to a time when they performed well. Single events are virtually meaningless in determining knowledge, skills and abilities. Patterns of performance must be identified before concluding that an applicant has specific qualifications.

Imagine that you're hiring a physician for the job we outlined in Chapter 8. The behavioral interview questions below are designed to assess applicants' ability to fulfill the following job requirement:

Takes complete patient history, including events leading to current visit, prior illnesses and other relevant information.

1. *Describe the process you and your organization used in your last job to ensure that you received all the information you needed to successfully treat each patient.*

2. *Did you use a computer in the process? Describe the tasks you had to perform with the computer.*

3. *What information did you collect from every patient? Did you write the information down or did you use other methods?*

4. *For each item on this list, please describe the method you would normally use to collect the information.*

5. *What kinds of patients created the biggest challenges to getting correct information?*

6. *Outline the approach you took to address these challenges.*

7. *Did you ever have to collect information from patients who did not speak English? How did you do this? Please provide me specific examples.*

8. *In the course of your career, what has been some of the damage you saw created by not having complete, accurate and timely information?*

9. *What are some of the things that you have done to avoid such occurrences?*

The preceding questions are just a sample of what could be asked. There are, of course, many more possible questions. An applicant's answers to a series of questions such as these provide robust and diverse information for making good hiring decisions. You will find significant variation in the quality of responses to a battery of questions such as this—that is exactly what you are looking for.

Situational Interview Questions

These questions are similar to behavioral interview questions. They do not, however, reference past performance. Instead, they ask applicants to describe how they would handle specific situations that are likely to occur. Situational interview questions are valuable when applicants are unlikely to have experienced what they will experience on the job for which they are applying. The strength of situational interview questions is that they allow us to see if applicants have the knowledge to handle situations that are likely to arise.

Situational interview questions do have limitations. An interview I had early in my career illustrates these limitations.

I was being interviewed for a job to supervise behavioral therapists that worked with special needs children. In the interview, I was asked the following situational question: "What would you do if you saw a child banging his head against a cement floor?" Although never before confronted with such a situation, my background and instincts allowed me to quickly respond that I would immediately put a pillow under the child's head. That was a pretty good answer. Still, the quality of my answer was misleading because talking about it in this calm setting did not reflect what I would have done under real pressure: run around in a panic looking for someone competent to take charge of the situation.

Situational interview questions are useful, but, unlike behavioral questions, they do not address how the applicant has actually performed.

The following battery of situational questions is for the same performance requirement assessed through behavioral questions in the last section. You should see the limitations of situational questions when compared to behavioral ones; they don't have the advantage of being able to dig into experience. Once again, the performance requirement is:

Takes complete patient history, including events leading to current visit, prior illnesses and other relevant information.

1. *Can you describe what you believe to be the ideal process for collecting all the information needed to successfully treat a patient?*

2. *If you had to use a computer, would you be able to do so?*

3. *What information needs to be collected from every patient? What is the best way capture this information?*

4. *I'm going to give you a list of the kinds of information we collect. For each item, describe the method you would use to collect the information.*

5. *Describe how you would collect information from patients who are in too much pain to speak. How about from patients who can't speak English? How about from very young children?*

6. *What damage do you think can be done by not having complete, accurate and timely information?*

7. *What are some of the things that you believe you can do to avoid such occurrences?*

Skills Tests

A skills test requires applicants to demonstrate their job skills. Like good interview questions, a skills test should closely reflect the skills required for the job.

For example, if you are hiring a PC technician, a good test is to have each applicant repair a broken computer. An appropriate assessment would evaluate the quality of the repairs and how long it took each applicant to make the repairs. For our physician job, we might give the applicant a neurological reflex hammer and ask him to demonstrate his skills in using this diagnostic instrument.

Questions and tests should be difficult enough so that you can differentiate among great, good and mediocre qualifications. If a job requirement can be learned in a day or two on the job, it usually does not make sense to test for that knowledge or skill.

Use the Selection Process

Step 1:   Schedule and conduct your interviews and skills assessments. Take the first five or ten minutes to describe the organization, the work environment, and then the job itself.

Step 2:   Really dig into each applicant's resume. Get as much information about his or her background as you possibly can. You are entitled to know why an applicant left prior jobs. Don't hesitate to ask what "personal reasons" means when it is indicated as the reason for leaving a prior job. Use probing questions throughout the interview, especially when going through the resume. There is a wealth of information to be had about what applicants did and how well they did it. For jobs that require strong cognitive abilities, ask about their grade point average in school. Delve into how they have had to think in their prior jobs.

Look for indicators of personality and motivation. Do this throughout the interview process.

Once, I interviewed an applicant for a customer service position. This applicant told me that she didn't agree with her present company's policy of giving credit cards to people with disabilities. She asked me with a sneer, "What do those people need credit cards for?" After that response, relative to the requirements for this customer service job, I had all the information I needed about her character.

As for motivation, there is a lot of information you can get that will give you insight into how motivated applicants are. Have they worked long hours regularly? Did they ever work full-time and also go to school? Did they have good grades? Did they travel far for a job? Will this job pay more than their last job? Those are just a few of many indicators that can help you determine if an applicant is motivated to perform well.

Step 3:   Take good notes, but keep them short and descriptive. You don't want to make applicants feel unnecessarily uncomfortable by keeping your head down, writing away. Summarize your notes after the interview. It's sometimes a good idea to wait a day before doing this. It gives you more time to think about the applicant's answers.

After you summarize your notes, destroy them. Once you have turned those notes into summaries, they have no more use. You or others may misinterpret them in the future.

Step 4:   Compare the strengths and weaknesses of each applicant. Have reference/background checks done on the applicants that you are seriously considering. There is a lot of important information that can be gotten from past bosses and from checking into an applicant's criminal history.

Step 5:   Hire the best candidate for the job. Pay the new employee based on market value. Do not structure a starting salary based on the applicant's prior wages. Such an approach seems logical, but it has a disparate impact on females and minorities.

Advanced Concepts

Intelligence Testing

Research has shown that intelligence is the best predictor of job success. There are a number of tests on the market that provide measures of intelligence, some of which are useful in making hiring decisions. Although organizations may find intelligence testing useful, there are psychometric and legal issues to consider.

Validity and reliability are two of the most prominent psychometric issues in testing of any kind. Legal issues are, perhaps, of even greater concern in employment testing. The use of intelligence tests could unfairly, even illegally, discriminate against some groups.

Personality Testing

Despite the appeal of gaining insight into applicants' personalities, the value of personality tests is limited in the employee selection process. Personality is important to job success, but defining and measuring personality is very difficult. Another issue to consider is that the constraints of some jobs and work environments can severely limit the impact of personality. Although still a concern, legal issues are less a concern in personality testing than they are in intelligence testing.

Most researchers in the field agree that the Five Factor Model of Personality provides the best available measurement of personality. If an organization were considering the use of personality tests, using one of the well-researched instruments based on the Five Factor Model would be advisable.

A well-structured interview and skills assessment process can provide some useful information about an applicant's intelligence and personality. These measures may not be as robust as those used by the highest-quality tests, but they are often good enough.

If your organization does choose to use cognitive ability or personality tests, you should consult Tests in Print and The EEOC Uniform

Guidelines to Employee Selection as you begin your search for the right test. It would then be wise to engage someone with an advanced degree in organizational or industrial psychology to conduct research and make recommendations.

Job and Organization Fit

Regardless of applicants' knowledge, skills, talents and personality, they still need to be a good fit for the job and the organization.

Job fit is a comparison of the characteristics of the job with the characteristics of each applicant. Organizational fit compares the characteristics of each applicant with the organization's *"personality."*

Identifying the characteristics of a job and, even more so, the "personality" of the organization are important and revealing exercises. They do, however, require systematic, honest and tenacious approaches to ensure that honest views rather than wishful thinking drive the processes. The information derived from such exercises can help organizations identify applicants who will thrive and those who will not. Senior management must drive the process of identifying the organization's personality.

CHAPTER TAKE-AWAY

Humans have potent instincts for selecting companions, but must overcome these instincts when it comes to hiring employees. You do this by using a simple, powerful and practical employee selection process. The process must use well-structured behavioral interview questions, situational interview questions and skills assessments. This is the best way to ensure that only highly qualified employees will be added to your payroll.

Final Thoughts
and the Road Ahead

A s the examples in this book have shown, merely *looking* like a leader does not a leader make. We have gone far too long on the assumption that leaders are qualified for the job merely because they happen to be in a leadership position. There is little evidence to support this assumption. On the contrary, both history and current events suggest that the opposite is true; leaders are often not qualified for the jobs they hold.

One of the lesser known, but most successful of all 20th Century CEOs was Darwin Smith, Chairman and CEO of Kimberly Clark Corporation from 1971 to 1991. When reflecting upon the key to his great success, he said, "I never stopped trying to become qualified for the job." This humble perspective is, perhaps, the most useful one that all modern leaders can hold. Jim Collins provides additional insight into this great business

leader and many others in *Good to Great,* one this text's recommended resources.

Build Real Leadership

The solutions outlined in this book are based on universal principles of performance that have been around for as long as humans have inhabited this planet. They also have been avoided and ignored by far too many for far too long.

If the goal is to be truly great at supervision, then you and your organization will achieve that goal by learning and applying what is outlined in this book. What makes for great supervision will not change next year, next century, or ever. So I urge you to avoid "flavor of the month" approaches and, instead, to learn and apply the knowledge, skills and methods of real supervision. Those who you lead deserve nothing less.

The Supervision Solution

The first chapter of this book discussed the myth and the truth of leadership. Now it is time for you to decide whether you are going to be the myth or the truth.

The following page provides a map to *The Supervision Solution*. As you and your organization do the work needed to make each box a reality, you move closer to *The Supervision Solution*. You won't get there overnight, but it can be a fast, challenging and rewarding journey. Follow the leadership and performance principles outlined in this book, and you'll do well. Challenge yourself, but don't be too hard on yourself, and get some assistance when you need it. Remember that great supervision requires both individual and group efforts. You can't do it alone.

Thank you for allowing me to be a part of your development as a supervisor. I wish you all the best as you and your organization learn and apply *The Supervision Solution*.

The Road to the Supervision Solution

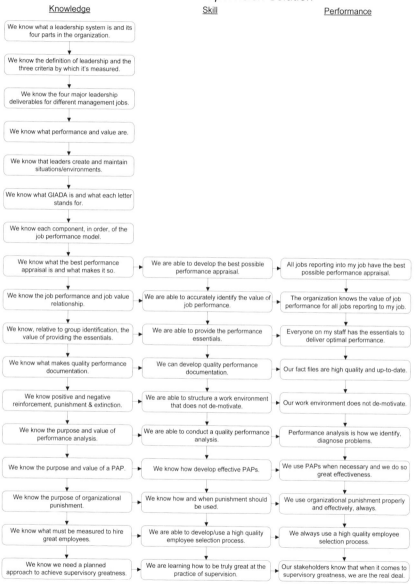

DEFINITIONS

Ability: the capability to perform (without skills).

Balanced Scorecard: An organizational leadership system that manages performance along four dimensions: financial performance, customer performance, business process performance and employee performance.

Behavior: The observable actions of a living organism.

Behavioral interview questions: Questions that test applicants on how they have applied their knowledge and skills in past situations.

CEO: Chief Executive Officer, the highest ranking job in a company.

Cost-effectiveness: The balance between using resources and achieving something of value.

Costs: Resources that are used to achieve something of value.

Effectiveness: Performance that is of value.

Emotion: A psychological reaction, often to environmental stimuli.

Extinction: A decrease in the frequency of behavior because there is no associated consequence.

Fact file: A log created by a supervisor to remember employee performances. That information is used to generate a performance appraisal.

GIADA: A universal problem-solving method: goal, information, analysis, decision and action.

Goal: A desired outcome.

Groupthink: When members of a group avoid conflict by withholding viewpoints that are contrary to that of the group.

Knowledge: the understanding of how something is supposed to be performed.

Leader: Someone that people follow.

Leadership system: A uniform set of skill, tools and methods by which the leaders of an organization drive performance.

Leadership: The quality of a leader's work.

Management: The cost-effective use of resources.

Manager: A person who works in management. It is also used as specific job title.

Negative reinforcement: An increase in the frequency of behavior due to the avoidance of something undesirable.

Objective: A milestone on the road to the goal. It must be specific, measurable, achievable, relevant and time-framed.

Organization: A social entity that is designed to achieve goals, cost-effectively use resources and provide value to its stakeholders.

Outcome: The result of something. It often follows an action or set of actions.

Performance achievement plan (PAP): A written plan to move a component of required job performance from an unacceptable level to an acceptable one.

Performance analysis: An investigatory process to determine the cause of performance problems, their impact and the most cost-effective cure.

Performance appraisal: A measure of past behaviors and outcomes.

Performance: Work behaviors and outcomes.

Personality: The psychological character and traits of a person.

Policies: The rules by which members of the organization are required to abide.

Positive reinforcement: An increase in the frequency of behavior due receiving something of value.

Punishment: A decrease in the frequency of behavior due to its association with something undesirable.

Situational interview questions: Questions that test applicants based upon situations that may occur on the job.

Skill: the actual ability to perform.

Stakeholders: Those people who have a vested interest in the performance of an organization. They include shareholders, customers, suppliers, employees, the community, etc.

Supervision: The management of employee performance.

Supervisor: A person charged with the responsibility of managing the performance of others.

Task analysis: A diagram that shows the sequence of steps necessary to perform a task. It typically also includes the knowledge, skills and tools needed for each step.

Trait: A psychological or physical component of an individual.

Value: The worth or importance of something.

SUGGESTED RESOURCES

A lthough the value of each resource provided here is directly relevant to the chapter under which it is listed, most all of the resources have applicability to a number of concepts discussed in this book.

Chapter 1: The Myth and the Truth of Leadership

Bossidy, L., Charan, R. (2002). *Execution: The Discipline of Getting Things Done*. New York: Crown Business.

Collins, J. (2001). *Good to Great*. New York: HarperCollins.

Collins, J., Porras, J. (1994). *Built to Last*. New York: HarperBusiness.

Drucker, P. (1973). *Management: Tasks, Responsibilities, Practices*. New

York: HarperCollins.

Holton, B. (1999). *Leadership Lessons of Robert E. Lee.* New York: Gramercy.

Chapter 2: The Measures of Leadership

Drucker, P. (2004). "What Makes an Effective Leader." *Harvard Business Review, Jun,* 58-63.

Goodwin, D. (2005). *Team of Rivals: The Political Genius of Abraham Lincoln.* New York: Simon & Schuster.

Kaltman, A. (1998). *Cigars, Whiskey & Winning: Leadership Lessons from General Ulysses S. Grant.* New Jersey: Prentice Hall Press.

Martin, R. (2007). "How Successful Leaders Think" *Harvard Business Review, Jun,* 60-67.

Quinn, R., (2005). "Moments of Greatness: Entering the Fundamental State of Leadership." *Harvard Business Review, Jul,* 74-83.

Chapter 3: The Concept of a Leadership System

Drucker, P. (1998). *On the Profession of Management.* Massachusetts: Harvard Business School Books.

Ragone, N. (2005). *Essential American Government*: Massachusetts: F+W Publications.

Roberts, J. (1993). *History of the World.* New York: Oxford University Press.

Chapter 4: The Organization's Leadership System

Kaplan, R., Norton, D. (2005). "The Balanced Scorecard: Measures That Drive Performance." *Harvard Business Review, Jul,* 172-180.

Kaplan, R., Norton, D. (2000). *The Strategy-Focused Organization: How Balanced Scorecard Companies Thrive in the New Business Environment*. Massachusetts: Harvard Business School Press.

Kaplan, R., Norton, D. (1996). *Balanced Scorecard: Translating Strategy into Action*. Massachusetts: Harvard Business School Press.

Chapter 5: What Business Leaders Manage

Anthony J. Rucci, Steven P. Kirn, and Richard T. Quinn. (1998). "The Employee-Customer-Profit Chain at Sears." *Harvard Business Review Jan*, 82-97.

Goden, S. (1999). *Permission Marketing*. New York: Simon and Schuster.

Dolan, R., Dobscha, S., Fournier, S., Moon, Y., Mick, D., Rangan, V. (2002). *Marketing Strategy: Business Fundamentals from Harvard School Publishing*. Massachusetts: Harvard School Publishing.

Porter, M. (1998). *On Competition*. Massachusetts: Harvard Business School Press Book.

Chapter 6: Great Leadership Changes Situations

Immaculee, I. (2006). *Left to Tell: Discovering God Amidst the Rwandan Holocaust*. California: Hay House.

Kotter, J. (2007). "Leading Change: Why Transformational Efforts Fail." *Harvard Business Review. January*, 96-102.

Beer, M., Eisenstat, R., Spector, B. (1990). "Why Change Programs Don't Produce Change." *Harvard Business Review, 68(6)*, 158-166.

Pascale, R., Sternin, J. (2005). "Your Company's Secret Change Agents." *Harvard Business Review. May*, 72-81.

Samuelson, R. (1988). "Status Quo Bias in Decision Making." *Journal of Risk and Uncertainty, Mar,* 7-59.

Zimbardo, P., (2007). *The Lucifer Effect.* New York: Random House Publishing.

Chapter 7: The Universe's Problem-solving Method: GIADA

Chet Richards, C. (2004). *Certain to Win.* Pennsylvania: Xlibris Corporation.

Locke, E., Latham, G. (1984). *Goal Setting: A Motivational Technique That Works!* New York: Prentice Hall.

Chapter 8: The Best Possible Performance Appraisal

Campbell, J. Dunnette, M., Arvey, R., Hellerviork, L. (1973). "The Development and Evaluation of Behaviorally Based Rating Scales." *Journal of Applied Psychology, 57,* 15-22.

Feldman, J. (1981). "Beyond Attribution Theory: Cognitive Processes in Performance Appraisal." *Journal of Applied Psychology, 55,* 127-148.

Flanagan, J. (1954). "The Critical Incident Technique." *Psychological Bulletin, 51,* 327-358.

Heilman, M. and Stopeck, M. (1985). "Being Attractive, Advantage Or Disadvantage? Performance Based Evaluations and Recommended Personnel Actions as a Function of Appearance, Sex and Job Type." *Organizational Behavior and Human Decision Processes, 35,* 202-215.

Howard, P., Howard, J. (2001). *The Owners Manual for Personality at Work.* Texas: Bard Press.

Latham, G., Wexley, K. (1977). "Behavioral observation scales for performance appraisal purposes." *Personnel Psychology, 30*, 255-268.

Mager, R. (1997). *Making Instruction Work*. Georgia: The Center for Effective Performance.

Morrow, P., McElroy J., Stamper B., Wilson, M. (1990). "The Effects of Physical Attractiveness and Other. Demographic Characteristics on Promotion Decisions." *Journal of Management, 16*, 723-736.

Chapter 9: The Value of Job Performance

Huselid, M., Beatty, R., Becker, B. (2005). "A Players or A Positions? The Strategic Logic of Workforce Management." *Harvard Business Review, Dec*, 110-117.

Brockbank, W., Ulrich, D. (2005). *The HR Value Proposition*. Massachusettes: Harvard Business School Publishing.

Chapter 10: Providing Employees with What They Need to Perform

Alexrod, A. (1999). *Patton on Leadership: Strategic Lessons for Corporate Warfare*. New Jersey: Prentice Hall.

May, G., Kahnweiler, W. (2000). "The Effect of a Mastery Practice Design on Learning and Transfer in Behavior Modeling Training." *Personnel Psychology, 53(2)*, 353-373.

Wagner, S., Parker, C., and Christiansen, N. (2003). "Employees That Think and Act Like Owners: Effects of Ownership Beliefs and Behaviors on Organizational Effectiveness." *Personnel Psychology, 56(4)*, 847-871.

Chapter 11: Documenting Performance

Howard, P. (2000). *The Owner's Manual for the Brain*. Texas: Bard Press.

Chapter 12: Motivated Employees Do Not Have To Be Motivated

Asch, S. (1955). "Opinions and Social Pressure." *Scientific American, 193(5)*, 31-35.

Komaki J, Waddell W., Pierce, M. (1977). "The Applied Behavior Analysis approach and individual employee: Improving performance in two small businesses." *Organizational Behavior and Human Performance, 19*, 337-352.

Latham, G. (2001). "The importance of understanding and changing employee outcome expectancies for gaining commitment to an organizational goal." *Personnel Psychology 2001, 54(3)*, 707-716.

Luthans F, Stajkovic A. (2000). "Provide recognition for performance improvement." *Academy of Management Executive, 13*, 40-57.

Milgram, S. (1963). "Behavioral Study of Obedience." *Journal of Abnormal and Social Psychology, 67(4)*, 371–378.

Organ, D., Bateman, T. (1991). *Organizational Behavior*. Illinois: Richard Irwin.

Chapter 13: Analyzing Job Performance Problems

Mager, R., Pipe, P. (1997). *Analyzing Performance Problems*. Georgia: Center for Effective Performance.

Chapter 14: Resolving Job Performance Problems

Solso, R. (1995). *Cognitive Psychology*. Massachusettes: Allyn & Bacon.

Chapter 15: Punishment

Baron-Cohen, S. (1991). "Precursors to a theory of mind: Understanding attention in others." In A. Whiten, Ed., *Natural Theories of Mind: Evolution, Development, and Simulation of Everyday Mind-reading (233-251).* Massachusetts: Basil Blackwell.

Scheff, T. "Shame in Self and Society." http://www.soc.ucsb.edu/faculty/scheff/3.html.

Chapter 16: Hiring Employees that Provide Needed Value

Huffcutt, A., Weekley, J., Wiesner, W., Degroot, T., Jones, C. (2001). "Comparison of Situational and Behavior Description Interview Questions for Higher-Level Positions" *Personnel Psychology 54(3),* 619–644.

Hunter, J., Schmidt, F., Judiesch, M. (1990). "Individual Differences in Output Variability as a Function of Job Complexity." *Journal of Applied Psychology, 75(1),* 28-42.

Kristof-Brown, A., Zimmerman, R., Johnson, E. (2005). "Consequences of Individuals' Fit at Work: A Meta-Analysis of Person-Job, Person-Organization, Person-Group, and Person-Supervisor Fit." *Personnel Psychology, 58(2),* 281-342.

Tziner, A., Joanis, C., Murphy, K. (2000). "A Comparison of Three Methods of Performance Appraisal with Regard to Goal Properties, Goal Perception, and Ratee Satisfaction." *Group & Organization Management, 25(2),* 175-190.

Additional Resources

Bolman, L., Deal, T. (1997). *Reframing Organizations.* California: Jossey-Bass.

Coram, R. (2002). *The Fighter Pilot Who Changed the Art of War.* New York: Little Brown.

Latham, G. (2007). "A speculative perspective on the transfer of behavioral science findings to the workplace: 'The times they are a-changin'." *Academy of Management Journal, 50(5),* 1027-1032.

Roberts, (1993). *History of the World.* New York: Oxford University Press.

Rynes, S. (2007) "Let's create a tipping point: What academics and practitioners can do, alone and together." *Academy of Management Journal, 50(5),* 1046-1054.

Stalk, G, Lachenauer, R. (2004). *Hardball: Are you Playing to Win?* Massachusetts: Harvard Business School Press.

Zhisui, L. (1994). *The Private Life of Chairman Mao.* New York, Random House.

INDEX